MW00414516

THE PROSPERITY LOOP

A Wealth Creation Model for Socially Conscious Leaders, Their Teams, and Their Communities

CHRIS LAUTENSLAGER

Published by Redwood Publishing, LLC
Orange County, California
www.redwooddigitalpublishing.com

ISBN: 978-1-956470-49-9 (hardcover)
ISBN: 978-1-956470-50-5 (paperback)
ISBN: 978-1-956470-51-2 (e-book)
ISBN: 978-1-956470-52-9 (audiobook)

Library of Congress Cataloguing Number: 2022913075

Cover Design: Michelle Manley of Graphique Designs, LLC
Interior Design: Jose Pepito
Editor: Avery Auer

Author Photo Credit: Chaz Ebert

First Edition. Printed in the United States of America.

To my mom and dad;
my brothers, Mike and Curtis;
and my sister, Ann.
I remember and miss each of you.

CONTENTS

FOREWORD

WHEN I WAS GROWING UP, I would listen in on the conversations my parents and the other "grown-ups" around me were having. Topics covered often included a local sports team (the haphazard Cubs or bungling Bears), neighborhood gossip, or situations at work. Then, every once in a while, I would inevitably hear them talk admiringly about that person who was a "self-made millionaire"—someone who had started with nothing and worked their way up the ladder of success rung by rung. It seemed apparent to me from the tone of my father's voice as he spoke about them that he admired these people. As I leaned into those conversations, thus began my dream of becoming a "self-made millionaire" myself.

For most of my life, I was a firm believer in self-sufficiency. I had convinced myself that the pathway to riches was individually crafted through the twin pillars of getting a good education and working hard. At twenty-eight, I made my first million dollars. I was wholly convinced that I had done it all on my own, despite my two business partners and a dozen employees. At the time, I believed that the work I'd done was the sole reason for my achievement. Looking back, I find it somewhat amusing to see the self-centeredness and naivety of my youthful perspective. It was only when I learned the importance of personal interconnectedness and the fundamental truth that we thrive together that my journey to true prosperity began.

The story of "self-made millionaires" is make-believe. There is no such thing. The very concept of singular success is an oxymoron. None of us operates in a vacuum and can realize such achievements alone. Life happens to us on a personal basis and also on a collective basis. All of us have been impacted by the COVID-19 pandemic and its continuing ripple effects on our psyches, our finances, and our families. Regardless of what any one of us has lived through, there's no denying that we have all seen and felt a level of global grief that was previously unimaginable. We've all been affected in some unanticipated way, and the shock of those seismic shifts became suffocating for many. Some experienced pain that they never thought could exist—with parents, spouses, siblings, children, and friends lost. There was the devastation of businesses and jobs lost, dishing out large portions of financial heartache for so many, coupled with a side of sorrow, anger, or numbing uncertainty of what lay ahead. Through this, arguably one of the toughest times any of us have experienced, we come to see yet again that one of the most important lessons is that none of us can endure or thrive alone. There must be mutual respect, trust, integrity, and collective purpose in order to achieve collective prosperity.

In my four decades of working in the business world, I have been a partner in several small firms (some successful, some not). I've held senior sales management and finance positions at some of the world's most prestigious financial institutions. I have witnessed and experienced the immense benefits of shared success and the devastating failures of self-centered, managerial greed. I have seen the implications of company policies driven solely by the bottom line, without regard for people. The impact of negative ripple effects within the organizations and communities was apparent and avoidable.

The Prosperity Loop is a contribution inspired by my life's career and business journey, designed to support yours. Every principle herein is based on lessons that ultimately changed the direction of my life toward a happiness and freedom I had been chasing but had never obtained when my focus was fixed solely on wealth and success. What you'll find in these pages is a formula, a model, and a movement for building a virtuous ongoing loop of shared organizational success. This foundation for collective prosperity is designed to integrate and align individual integrity with professional integrity in a model in which investing in and developing others helps you as a leader in the success of your business!

There is an increasing number of CEOs and business leaders who are choosing to view the world through a different prism and a broader lens. Right now, you may be safely secluded in the cloister of your current business, but the truth is, you are not satisfied because you are a different breed of leader. You know something is very wrong with the effects of our economy. You know that today's system of capitalism is broken. You don't just want to get to the next level in your business; you also want to get to the next level in *life*. You want to operate in an environment that values honesty and integrity. You're a leader, but you recognize that you didn't get to where you are alone, nor are you going to get to where you want to be on your own.

It really does all start with you, but it doesn't end there. This work is about learning to trust, support, and acknowledge yourself and others. It's more foundational. It's about taking a long, hard look at your current persona. Does it build or damage the relationships in your life—your family, your friends, your colleagues, your peers? How you see other people, what your expectations are, and how you interact with them are what define who you are and what you'll become.

The Prosperity Loop is for the leader who aims to be part of the solution and who leans toward building a socially conscious organization, community, or society without abandoning the reality of operating a profitable business. It is for those who want to acknowledge, thank, and reward the people who keep the wheels of their organization turning and who have built the business to be what it is today. It is for those who want to shape an organization that celebrates a legacy of collaborative purpose and success. This is a call to action to change on a personal level in order to magnify the positive ripple effect you can create. It can also serve as a companion as you aim to support growing levels of engagement, accomplishment, and wealth creation for you, your people, your organization, and your community. This is not fantasy or some type of pie-in-the-sky communal model of socialism; organizational profits can indeed grow in tandem with personal happiness.

The cornerstone of my personal accomplishments and career trajectory was the understanding that my success was dependent on my collaboration with others. While this may sound like a fundamentally simple concept, it is the application of embracing others that is the foundation of achieving financial and personal prosperity. In this book, you will find the tools that create collective prosperity—those which I discovered along my journey. You'll have access to viable methods for executing the organizational, cultural, and personal changes needed as you shift to a structural model of shared success. You'll read the stories of companies that embrace and reward those who've contributed to their success—employees at all levels. You'll see how, from an organizational standpoint, this work is about improving employee satisfaction, retention, and productivity and how investing in your employees can measurably enhance your company's bottom-line performance. You'll learn how shared success provides a richness to life in addition to the financial reward you've earned as a leader, and you'll discover how you can experience this richness in your own life.

My path in life has not been paved in gold, nor has my journey been perfectly planned or linear in growth. I had to learn to fully embrace the imperfections of the process and the roads I chose to reach each point of discovery. The same holds true for each and every one of us, as the lessons along our journeys to success will help guide the development of our own "Prosperity Loop."

There are four critical benefits to be realized as a result of your adaptation of the Prosperity Loop for yourself and your organization:

1. You will experience joy and prosperity as part of the foundation of your life.
2. You will build sustainable happiness and prosperity for employees, families, and communities.

3. You will develop stronger relationships, a higher level of integrity, and a greater sense of shared purpose.
4. You will expand your impact through the increase in growth and profitability of your company.

Whether you are seeking personal enhancement or improvement in the performance of your company, *The Prosperity Loop* provides a strategic foundation, the principles, and the questions required for organizations to shift to a healthier *shared* experience of success and the resultant creation of wealth. You can lead a company in which profitability occurs through the prioritization of the people who helped make it happen. Welcome to a means of doing more for the collective good and being happier as a whole.

"FOLLOW THE MONEY"

I'M WINNING; YOU'RE LOSING. That was the cultural philosophy that ran like wildfire through the floors of the Chicago Mercantile Exchange (CME) when my brother Curtis and I made our debut as derivatives traders in the 1980s. It was electric, providing a rush of sensory overload the instant we walked onto the trading floor. Being a trader was the perfect means to do precisely what we hungered for: become rich! Every day, we stepped into a highly physical mano-a-mano ring fueled with endless jostling for supremacy, brute intimidation, and relentless, full-throated yelling. There was no subterfuge, no decorum, and the free-for-all environment was fueled by testosterone and fury. Everyone was fighting to be heard, and we were all in it to win.

Any person who has ever traded on the floor of a commodity exchange would likely agree that the best description of the experience is from Dan Aykroyd playing Louis Winthorpe III, the businessman working for the commodities brokerage Duke & Duke in the 1983 movie *Trading Places.* Louis says the following to his partner, Billy Ray Valentine (Eddie Murphy):

> Well, this is it, the last bastion of pure capitalism left on Earth. . . . Think big. Think positive. Never show any sign of weakness. Always go for the throat. Buy low; sell high. Fear? That's the other guy's problem. Nothing you have ever experienced will prepare you for the unbridled carnage you are about to witness. The Super Bowl, the World Series—they don't know what pressure is. In this building, it's either kill or be killed. You make no friends in the pits, and you take no prisoners. One minute, you're up half a million in soybeans, and the next—*boom*—your kids don't go to college, and they've repossessed your Bentley.

Curtis was the only person I felt I could trust down in the trenches. In truth, he was the only person I trusted anywhere. We began our careers trading Japanese Yen futures and options, and we were true brothers, always making sure the other was OK. Throughout the chaos of the day, we would periodically catch each other's eyes to check in. In that brief glance, we'd instantly know how the other was surviving (and *if* he was surviving). We'd also know whether the trading was good, bad, or terrifying. It was doubtful that anyone else could discern our moments of brotherly humanity amid the chaos of the money-driven world, which was a good thing because we could never have shown weakness in the pits, and we most certainly could *never* show fear. However, that didn't mean fear was not present.

Experiencing all facets of a career in commodities trading meant that there were times of sick-to-your-stomach, palm-sweating panic. One quick mistake, and you could lose everything of material value in your life. There were no do-overs down there. Kindness, consideration, and cooperation are normally considered to be helpful human values, but they would be exploited as vulnerabilities whenever possible. Our objective was crystal clear: The creation of wealth was the only thing that mattered. And the truth was, that suited my "self-made millionaire" quest just fine.

A few years before we started trading, Curtis and I had made a vow to never end up like our father. We had grown up watching him work long hours, building a business that became his pride and purpose. And then, from out of nowhere, his once thriving, family-owned construction company went bankrupt as a result of the Arab oil embargo. Decades of sacrifice and dedication had disappeared seemingly overnight. He could do nothing to stop it. After losing his business, his sense of self withered away, followed by the rest of his identity. Soon thereafter, he died of a stress-induced heart attack, and our thoughts about our lives, our world, and our futures changed forever.

In the period that followed my father's death, Curtis and I came to believe in an unpredictable, uncaring world that surrounded us. The loss of our father and his business spilled over into all aspects of our lives. We experienced the heartache of losing our family home, along with the uneasy and sorrowful glances that neighbors and friends tried to hide. Worst of all, we saw the crushing emotional impact it all had on our mother and sister. There was no bailout money or miracle rescue with a fairy-tale happy ending—just a sense of abandonment and recognition that *we were entirely on our own.*

As a family, we had never thought that such financial distress could happen to us. Experiencing that level of trauma as teenagers ingrained within my brother and me a fervent desire to make money. We had each seen the importance it had on our lives, but we approached the pursuit of self-driven monetary success in quite different ways. Curtis's response was to adopt a "live for today" attitude. Believing that life could end at a moment's notice, he figured he might as well embrace all that was available to him and do so as thoroughly as possible. He dropped out of college and began traveling worldwide, surrounding himself with a posse of new friends. One month, he'd be whitewater rafting down the Colorado River; the next, he was touring Europe. He took in the Olympics in Lake Placid, Carnival in Rio de Janeiro, and the Super Bowl in New Orleans. His favorite saying became "There's always room for more fun," and his magnetic personality seemed to pull rich people and lucrative opportunities into his life almost effortlessly.

My response was the polar opposite, as I opted to put my nose to the grindstone and work hard to be prepared for the worst. I focused on my education, graduating with honors from the University of Colorado and then earning my MBA from Northwestern University. I ingested everything associated with business, with the objective of becoming successful and wealthy. I consumed the theories of Adam Smith for breakfast, Joseph Schumpeter for lunch, and Milton Friedman for dinner. I was a hungry student learning about the invisible hand's countless benefits, and I quickly became "Mr. Free Market." To me (and my business school educators and peers), the virtues of capitalism were obvious, plentiful, and increasingly in vogue—and it was a trend I was happy to ride.

When Curtis and I first started working on the floor of the CME, we both longed to be rich, independent, and surrounded by the accoutrements associated with status. Our "might is right" attitude served us well as we built our business, hiring traders, brokers, and clerks to expand our operations into other trading pits. Soon enough, we were on top of the world and well on our way, with nothing ahead of us but a glide path to greater riches. Then the world changed again.

In 1992, the CME introduced the first electronically traded futures contract on its Globex system. Traders were assured by CME management that floor trading would never be negatively impacted, and the consensus within the commodities industry was that nothing could replace the efficiencies of floor trading. Curtis viewed the new technology as a fad; I considered it the end of our livelihoods, with my fears about money starting to return and filling me with dread. I could sense the world was changing, and I was anxious about what that might mean.

During this period of uncertainty, I met a wonderful woman named Cynthia and fell in love. We dated, I proposed, she accepted, and we set a date to be married. She was from New Jersey and wanted to move back East. It was an idea that suited me just fine, as her family had deep ties to Wall Street, and the allure of even greater riches was a siren song that rang out in my favor. Within a year, it became obvious to me. The CME trading floor was destined for an early demise, and the tides of change were pushing me to Wall Street.

Cynthia and I readied ourselves to leave Chicago and begin building a new life together in New York City. The day after my wedding, I embraced Curtis and said goodbye as we cried both tears of joy and sadness. We had been through so much together, but it was time for each of us to begin anew. It was difficult, confusing, and heartbreaking. As our taxi pulled away, I caught a glimpse of Curtis's eyes. They looked empty and devoid of emotion. Two weeks later, he shot himself and died.

There are times in life that can be impossible to comprehend. Losing Curtis was yet another of those times for me. I had believed that I'd already been tested by life and could face any and every challenge. I survived physical and sexual abuse in my childhood; the murder of my older brother, Mike; the premature death of my dad; financial adversity; and my mom's crippling stroke with the challenges of her caretaking responsibilities. Hadn't I already been through enough? But the level of grief and guilt I felt with Curtis's passing was almost insurmountable. Life seemed cruel, and I felt so very alone.

It took decades of towering highs and extremely difficult lows to realize that I had learned the wrong lesson when my father died. I came to clearly see that it wasn't the loss of money that had led to his ultimate demise; it was his lack of a broader purpose and personal support, which could have sustained him during a period of great trauma. From the day my father died, I had been set adrift of any moorings, and my guiding philosophy had become a combination of "Whatever it takes," "Might is right," and "Let the chips fall where they may." It wasn't until my own life started to spiral out of control and I felt as powerless as my father that I learned a better formula for living. Only out of a sense of desperation was I open to building a new approach to life: a life that was free from the fear and pain associated with the singular pursuit of money.

At that moment, I made the choice to embrace the collective prosperity of helping others.

For many, it's not until the earthquake shatters the illusions of their life that they realize just how fragile their world can be. It is easy to believe that you are above the fray. However, we all have the ability to create a solid foundation that we can always count on: one based on our relationships. That's why there will never be a better time than now to do what is morally right. Our lives are a series of "right here, right now, today" moments. And in the present moment, you can choose to be the leader who walks among your people and leads alongside them in the name of pursuing a purpose of collective prosperity.

RESHAPING CAPITALISM

WHO IS IN CHARGE HERE?! That's the essential question of how economics works. Capitalism is based on the premise that individuals know what's best for themselves. It allows people to reap the rewards (and consequences) of their efforts and ventures without the government intervening to determine winners, losers, and who gets how much. It is this individualization of incentives that consistently creates the brilliance of innovation and the advancement of mankind. It is also this individualization that creates opportunities for people and companies to abuse basic responsibilities to others in pursuit of ever-greater personal rewards.

Socialism proposes that government can rise above the base desires of individuals to create a greater good for everyone. After all, socialist-type government policies were responsible for creating the interstate transportation system, providing for our national defense, and establishing an electric grid system that illuminated the country.

However, when government bureaucrats make decisions on how to allocate specific public resources (property, funding, production rights, etc.), it is inevitable that politics determine winners and losers as part of the process. And regrettably, many governments have a long and well-documented track record of corruption, mismanagement, and waste that interferes with the best of intentions.

While many government-sponsored businesses are well-intentioned and support positive causes, they are seldom true builders of wealth.

I'm a capitalist, and I believe in the opportunities and possibilities that exist within capitalism. Trade between people, societies, and nations has existed since the dawn of time. Formal trade (the exchange of goods and services) can be traced to Mesopotamia as long ago as 2000 BC.[1] It has been the primary tool of commerce across the world and throughout history, supporting the growth of villages to empires. Capitalism has consistently demonstrated itself to be the best economic system to raise the living standards for millions of people.

Historically, in the business world, management's decisions were assumed to be based on the long-term interests of the company. Increasing profits, positive cash flow, limited debt levels, prudent investments in research and development, and capital expenditures were considered indicators of a well-managed firm, leading to rising stock prices. This may be a very simplified example; however, it is not an exaggeration to say that the perspective of corporate capitalism has, in too many cases, been reduced to a singular focus: increasing stock prices *regardless* of any potential consequences.

Examples of today's capitalistic insanity include nonsensical mergers and acquisitions, off-the-books accounting gimmicks, collateralization of junk debt, SPAC financing, accumulation of excessive debt, and IPOs based on fantasy instead of profits. These strategies are designed to increase stock prices, often by channeling funding into the previously illegal practice of stock buybacks. Companies are cannibalizing themselves strictly for the benefit of shareholders, as well as their willing partners in management and the board of directors.

This is not the only time capitalism was exploited by the powerful primarily for their benefit. During the Gilded Age, which lasted from the late 1860s to approximately 1896, the following took place:

1. Industry experienced unprecedented growth based on new technology.
2. A limited number of individuals capitalized on this new technology and quickly accumulated vast amounts of wealth.
3. Greedy, corrupt industrialists, bankers, and politicians enjoyed extraordinary wealth and opulence at the expense of the working class.
4. Middle-class Americans protested the rampant political corruption and social inequality.[2, 3]

The period following the Gilded Age offers examples of how the boundaries of capitalism were redefined to ensure a more balanced economic environment. Many Americans became inspired to use their political power to upset the rules that favored the special interests of the rich.

Today's blatant lack of fairness is not just about money and wealth; it is also about a moral erosion that is spreading throughout our society and undermining any sense of hope for the future.

Over the years, the "free market" concept for increasing shareholder value extolled by Milton Friedman in his 1962 book *Capitalism and Freedom* has been distorted, maligned, and abused.[4] Political economist Joseph Schumpeter's argument for the need for "creative destruction" to ensure efficient and innovative capital flows in his 1942 book *Capitalism, Socialism, and Democracy* likely never anticipated the human and societal devastation of large sections of America in offshoring entire industries.[5] His perspective was originally guided by the reallocation of resources to create additional investment and commerce for a nation, not the complete elimination of it. Adam Smith, one of the first well-known theorists on capitalism, touted the benefits of the "invisible hand," based on a marketplace that provided a level playing field for all participants.[6] However, he was deeply concerned about the potential for manipulation of markets and politicians by deep-pocketed oligopolists out for their singular benefit. In his 1776 book *The Wealth of Nations,* Smith states the following:

> Civil government, so far as it is instituted for the security of property, is in reality instituted for the defense of the rich against the poor, or of those who have some property against those who have none at all.[7]

There are many facets of business and capitalism that have become incredibly skewed—and not in favor of the individual:

- Many business decisions are driven by noneconomic political considerations. For example, there are tax incentives to allow private equity firms to purchase companies with massive amounts of debt even if it will be impossible for the company to repay.[8] There are bankruptcy and tax loopholes that incentivize management to sacrifice their employees' benefits and pensions for their own financial gain.[9] There are tax-avoidance structures that allow corporations to avoid paying taxes in their native countries.[10]
- Many are unaware that until 1979, there were usury laws in every state that prohibited borrowers from charging "predatory" interest rates above 8–10 percent.[11], [12] Today, credit card companies can legally charge any interest rate they want as long as it is legally disclosed.[13] Some credit cards charge up to 36 percent annual interest on outstanding debt balances, not including fees. That means your total amount of debt doubles every two years! Such a burdensome rate of interest has created modern debtors' prisons. A broad swath of private firms and public institutions are keeping millions of people chained to the harmful effects of debt enslavement.
- There are companies whose products do substantial harm while fostering profitability. Some products can cultivate loneliness and animosity and even fracture societies. Some products are produced by exploiting child labor in underdeveloped nations. We also see it when a business provides a service that purposely uses illegal, monopolistic business tactics to destroy competitive businesses. Creating a product or service used by billions does not

> validate *any* behavior. There have been many times when we have deemed the practices of a company harmful even though its products are popular.[14]

Throughout history, capitalism has been consistently manipulated for the benefit of just a few, often resulting in the suffering of others. The abuses of child labor, debtors' prisons, and slavery were all accepted parts of the economic system in their day. (Sadly, many of these horrible practices still exist in parts of the world. Eliminating these amoral behaviors is the reason we must redefine the laws of the capitalist model.) There is no denying the horrible legacy of these practices; concurrently, we need to recognize that the decisions to include these exploitative actions were made by people to pursue greater wealth at any cost.

It is now happening again. In a matter of decades, businesses once seen as the engines of dreams and the builders of futures are being spotlighted for their relentless, never-ending crusade for record profits. It's a drive for the bottom line that has come at the cost of sacrificing our well-being and humanity. Companies have strengthened their capacity to replace the middle class with the working poor: people who work full time yet are struggling to pay for the basic necessities of life, such as food, shelter, health care, and education. There is a term for this type of heartless and callous behavior: *greed.*

In the movie *Wall Street,* Michael Douglas plays Gordon Gekko, a successful private equity investor who argues passionately and convincingly that "Greed is good; greed works." His message is that the human drive to obtain wealth fosters innovation and makes the best use of resources. He's wrong. Greed is a sultry and insidious desire, one that can be easy to justify to oneself. After all, what's wrong with being an entrepreneur, working hard, and making a better life for you and the ones you love?

Companies that (and people who) embrace greed damage others in their pursuit and use of wealth. This is the Achilles' heel of capitalism, and there is significant harm associated with these practices, which are connected to but ignore the well-being and prosperity of all people. No longer can we continue to pretend that businesses operate in a vacuum that only involves their shareholders. It's beyond time we acknowledge businesses' broad impact on employees, families, neighborhoods, and society. Multiple times in our lifetimes, we have seen the collateral damage of jobs lost, savings disintegrated, communities abandoned, and lives destroyed.

Is it any wonder that an increasing number of Americans have lost faith in capitalism when there are so many glaring abuses of the system? When laws have been created and implemented based on a variety of political objectives that determine who the primary beneficiaries of capitalism will be, those laws do not always support the larger society (the people). In these cases, it is clear that the type of laws that are enacted and the way in which those laws are executed are (or have become) flawed.

Too often, we're brainwashed by the mantra that there is only one type of capitalism and that there must be winners and losers for the system to function correctly. Do not be seduced by this siren song of the status quo. There are leaders and organizations that prioritize providing good-paying jobs with benefits, partnering with vendors for jointly beneficial services, and proudly supporting local communities. There are examples of successes in the capitalist system that show us that any leader or business has choices available from which to choose.

It's not that capitalism doesn't work or that the drive to create a highly profitable organization is misguided. Quite the contrary! Companies can't exist without profits. However, this revision of capitalism, through the reprioritization of profits, will allow all Americans the opportunity to be justly rewarded for their contribution of productivity. It is imperative that we never discount or underestimate the significance of living by the philosophy that people have a higher value than the accumulation of "things."

It's time for us all to question whether or not we like what is happening in the United States today and decide if we are ready to be agents of change. The need for a significant shift in how and why we do business is apparent. All you need to do is look out and see employees contributing years of time, energy, and talent to the building of successful organizations and then being discarded like widgets that have reached their obsolescence date. By recognizing that we can change the boundaries within which capitalism can operate, we plant the seeds of possible solutions. The rules of business are not sacred or set in stone; they can be changed and restructured in response to the needs of society. *The Prosperity Loop* is a call to all those who see the potential for their business to be a catalyst for change.

WHAT'S ESSENTIAL?

WHAT'S ESSENTIAL, AND WHAT'S NONESSENTIAL? While working on Wall Street, I took my daughters to visit the house where I grew up in Chicago. As I drove up to my home for the first time in decades, I was surprised by how much smaller and humbler it was than I remembered. The current owners were gracious and excited to allow me to share my family's history with my daughters.

As I walked through the hallways of my old home, memories flooded my mind. I remembered how my two brothers and I had shared the same bedroom, sleeping on a triple bunk bed. My sister had her own room, which at the time seemed like an extravagance. The bedroom my parents shared was barely big enough for the current owners' bed and two dressers. Recounting my family's stories made me realize that growing up, I had always thought our home was that of a prosperous family. After all, we had a swimming pool in the backyard!

As we walked out back, I stopped in disbelief. That luxurious swimming pool I had loved throughout my childhood was still there, and it was, in reality, quite small. In fact, it was smaller than some of my current neighbors' front lawn fountains. I was dumbfounded by just how different my life and expectations were as I was growing up. My definition of what was essential had changed so much. My children were even more surprised than I was. What stood before us was such a different world than what they were accustomed to in their life of privilege. I felt a sadness wash over me, aware that my wife's and my desire as parents to care for them as best we could had simultaneously minimized their exposure to a broader perspective and definition of what was essential.

I thought about my neighbors from all those years ago. Mr. Beck hung draperies for Sears. Mr. Joya was a warehouse worker at Motorola. Mr. Gordini was a machinist at a factory, building nuts and bolts. The owner of the biggest house on the block was a cameraman at the public television station in Chicago. Everyone had a family with two to five kids. Some grandparents lived with them, and most moms didn't need to work in order to cover the monthly bills.

None of those families would be able to afford to live in those very same homes with those jobs and the associated earnings of today. It's not just that the cost of living has increased; it's also that the level of earnings for working families hasn't remotely kept pace with rising costs.

As a result of my having met, collaborated, and conversed with hundreds of Americans over the past few years, it has become acutely obvious to me that regardless of their location, race, education, income, and gender, they all believe the economic opportunities and upward mobility enjoyed by previous generations do not exist today. There are pockets of possibility for some, but not for the population at large. Many feel a fundamental lack of hope, and that is driving transformational change in our nation. And the organizational catalyst is clear to most: While employee productivity and company profits have skyrocketed over the last forty-plus years, workers have not been fairly compensated for their contributions to a company's success. In their singular pursuit of profits, businesses have sacrificed the middle class of America.

Arguably, at no other time in our lives have we felt the sting of a system that needs to change more than we have during the global COVID-19 outbreak. The great shake-up of the deadly pandemic has further highlighted and accelerated these revealing gaps of inequities and the need for broader change. A June 2020 journal article by Philip H. Mirvis titled "From Inequity to Inclusive Prosperity: The Corporate Role" highlights the impact of COVID-19 on revealing the economic inequality in America:

> The COVID-19 pandemic in the US has brought inequities into sharp relief. While most high-wage workers could shelter in place and work remotely from their homes, lower-wage workers faced a double jeopardy: disproportionate numbers of them were laid off and those who kept working, in health care, social services, and other "essential" businesses, were more apt to be exposed to the

> virus. African American and Hispanic workers (and their communities) suffered higher rates of infection and death as a function of exposure and underlying health disparities. As health official Dr. Fauci put it, the virus shines "a very bright light on some of the real weaknesses and foibles in our society."[15]

With information sharing at our fingertips in our modern world and the ease of communication through social networks, it's easy to see that millions of workers are being harmed and systemically abused within today's version of capitalism. We hear it in the stories of layoffs and employees who know they are not being fairly rewarded for their contributions to the creation of record profits. Concurrently, many are aware their companies' managements are coercing profits through actions such as artificially inflating stock prices to inordinately reward themselves (at the expense of employees and all others).

Molly Kinder is a fellow at the nonprofit public policy organization at the Brookings Institution and an adjunct professor at Georgetown University's McCourt School of Public Policy. In their essay "Windfall Profits and Deadly Risks," Kinder and her team examine what frontline retail workers earned during the pandemic versus what they could have earned based on their companies' significant increase in profits. Their analysis showed that the top retail companies earned on average an extra $16.9 billion in profit in 2020, a 39 percent increase from 2019. Their stock prices were up an average of 33 percent. With few exceptions, very little of this increased profitability was passed on to frontline retail workers.

Kinder and her team studied thirteen companies: Amazon, Walmart, Lowe's, Kroger, Best Buy, Home Depot, Target, Costco, Albertsons, Ahold Delhaize, Walgreens Boots Alliance, CVS Health, and Dollar General. These companies, on average, raised pay for their frontline workers by an average of just $1.11 per hour since the pandemic began, noting that this accounts for "a 10 percent increase on top of wages that are often too low to meet a family's basic needs." And at the time of the report, it had been 133 days since the retail workers in the analysis last received any hazard pay.[16]

INCREASE IN RETAILER PROFITS IN 2020

Company	Qs reported in 2020	2020 profits	2019 profits	$ change	% Change
		(in millions)			
Amazon	3	$17,377	$11,347	+$6,030	53%
Walmart	3	$15,601	$10,740	+$4,861	45%
Home Depot	3	$10,009	$8,761	+$1,248	14%
CVS Health	3	$6,206	$4,887	+$1,319	27%
Lowe's	3	$4,857	$3,771	+$1,086	29%
Target	3	$2,988	$2,447	+$541	22%
Costco	2	$2,227	$2,003	+$224	11%
Kroger	2	$2,031	$1,069	+$962	90%
Ahold Delhaize (U.S.)	3	$1,578*	$1,377*	+$201	15%
Dollar General	2	$1,438	$812	+$626	77%
Walgreens (U.S.)	2	$885*	$1,695*	-$810	-48%
Albertsons	2	$871	$344	+$527	153%
Best Buy	2	$591	$503	+$88	17%
TOTAL		**$66,659**	**$49,755**	**$16,903**	**39%**

* Operating income for the U.S. sectors of the company

Source: Company quarterly earnings as of November 2020

B Metropolitan Policy Program at BROOKINGS

Source: Molly Kinder, Brookings Metro

HAZARD OR ADDITIONAL PAY PAID TO EMPLOYEES OF RETAIL COMPANIES

Figure 6. Breakdown of COVID-19 compensation

COMPANY	COVID-19 COMPENSATION: total $ workers received during the pandemic				COVID-19 COMPENSATION
	HAZARD PAY: TEMPORARY COMPENSATION			*PERMANENT WAGE INCREASE*	
	Hourly wage increase	Regular bonuses	One-off bonuses (for full-time employees)	Permanent wage increase	
Best Buy	$2.50			$15/hr	$4,414
Home Depot		$100/week		Varied; ~$1.25/hr	$3,271
Target	$2		2 x $200	$15/hr	$3,200
Lowe's	$2		6 x $300		$2,143
Amazon	$2		1 x $500		$1,369
Kroger	$2		1 x $300; 1 x $400		$1,249
Albertsons	$2		1 x $160*		$1,200
Ahold Delhaize (U.S.)	Varied by chain, ~$1.25		Varied by chain		$1,075
Costco	$2				$1,040
Walmart			3 x $300		$900
Dollar General	~$1		~$100		$334
Walgreens (U.S.)			1 x $300		$300
CVS Health			1 x $300*		$300

* Bonus ranged from $150-$500 for hourly workers depending on position (pharmacist, manager, store associate, etc). From our analysis, a $300 bonus aligns with industry standard for a full-time cashier/store associate.

Methodology: Amount of temporary hourly increases and bonuses are from company websites. Total COVID-19 Compensation is the total amount a frontline essential worker who works 40hr/week would have made from hourly wage increases, regular bonus, one-off bonuses, and permanent wage increases. The amount earned from permanent wage increases is calculated using the starting wage or average wage for a cashier working 40hrs/week, excludes pandemic-related temporary wage increases. Calculated from when the company announced the increase through November 19, 2020.

Source: Brookings analysis of company COVID-19 Compensation between March 13, 2020 and November 19, 2020

B | Metropolitan Policy Program at BROOKINGS

Source: Molly Kinder, Brookings Metro

The stark numbers reveal a landscape where most large retailers continue to prioritize profits and wealth for shareholders over investments in their employees, even when their workers are exposed to an environment of greater risk. Only one company, Home Depot, spent more on pandemic pay than it earned in additional profit. On average, the six public companies in the study compensated workers at a rate that was less than half of the additional profit earned during the pandemic (over the previous year). The least generous companies were the ones posting the most significant profit growth on average. "Amazon and Walmart could have quadrupled the hazard pay they gave their frontline workers and still earned more profit than the previous year," said Kinder and her team.

There is no denying that companies and humans are strongly influenced by money, success, and prestige. However, the deeply personal connection to money and prestige can be transcended by prosperity-minded leadership. Leaders are increasingly recognizing the value of a broader, inclusive prosperity versus a myopic focus on profits. The pathway to prosperity and a better America is founded on a more just, shared remuneration of wealth.

JUST Capital is an independent nonprofit promoting the growth of "just" companies. They were co-founded in 2013 with the mission to "build an economy that works for all Americans by helping companies improve how they serve all their stakeholders—workers, customers, communities, the environment, and shareholders."[17] In one of its surveys in 2020, which engaged one thousand Americans, JUST Capital discovered that 77 percent believed that companies should provide hazard or additional pay to employees working in essential jobs. The same survey also found that almost nine in ten Americans agree that 2020 and the challenges therein have presented an opportunity for companies to hit "reset" and focus on doing right by their workers, customers, communities, and the environment. The majority of respondents agreed that we need a more evolved form of capitalism to tackle the shift. Only about a quarter of respondents believed that our current form of capitalism ensures the greater good of society, and a mere 29 percent believed it produces the kind of society they want for the next generation or felt it works for the average American.[18]

The most important lesson of the Prosperity Loop is the understanding that prioritizing people is not synonymous with sacrificing profits. This model is not an either-or proposition. The needs of stakeholders (such as employees, vendors, customers, and community members) and those of shareholders do not need to be considered disparate positions. It is not only possible but also advantageous to find common ground, to create winning compromises, to build a prosperous world. It all starts with a change in philosophy toward a more comprehensive perspective of rewarding value.

True richness comes from the life choices that create more than just wealth for oneself; it paints with a broader brush and leaves a more comprehensive footprint. By investing in the team members who help create success, we will be able to exponentially build remarkable solutions to shift the current dynamic of corporate America. When we look to a solution for reshaping capitalism, we need to begin by looking at our values and choices, both as individuals and as organizations.

The choices we make define our lives and encompass benefits, consequences, opportunities, possibilities, risks, and disappointments. They contain elements of essentialism and nonessentialism. How often do we genuinely take the time to acknowledge the category in which our decisions fall and their significance in our lives and in the lives of others?

In our modern times, where people without wealth are struggling to keep up with the cost of living, corporations need to move past the old mentality of cutting costs, wages, benefits, and community resources to save money. The incremental impacts of individual firms have become exponential within our society, increasing the divide between economic classes and magnifying the question of what is necessary.

What's essential? is the question we need to be asking given the daily life experiences we all have, regardless of age, gender, race, and political views. This is not an overstatement. The priorities and practices of the current business model must change.

We cannot wait for or solely depend on large companies to be the engine that drives change in our world. If there is going to be a shift in what's essential to businesses, that change will also have to come from the owners and CEOs of small and midsize enterprises, which employ the vast majority of Americans. It is SMEs that have the greatest potential to change our world.

TIME FOR THE KING TO BE DETHRONED

WHEN BUSINESS ENTITIES BECOME SO POWERFUL and reckless that they negatively impact millions of people, entire nations, or the whole world, there needs to be a societal rebuke to eliminate such threats. Sometimes that societal response can advance to the point of "revolution." We are in the middle of an economic revolution today. The shareholder-first, CEO-first pyramid of business is antiquated and not serving us as a modern, equality-seeking society wanting to find a way back to supporting one another *and* our community.

Our world is changing. We are asking for more—more equality, more integrity, more community. We are asking that the "kings" of business be dethroned and come walk among the people to understand and adjust to the needs of the everyday individual. We talk about systemic economic inequality, the disintegration of the middle class, and the need to make substantial strides to rectify what the division between the "kings" (CEOs and shareholders) and the "working people" of society has created. Systemic economic inequality is dividing the United States. People are in debt up to their ears and living in perpetual financial servitude. So much of this work is about preventing us from having a permanent underclass.

In my mind, there are two key drivers of business success: one is concerned with morality, the other with economics. Both are choices that can collectively benefit or injure others. Most business leaders seem to be solely focused on economic principles. Unless they learn to partner these economic principles with moral principles, it's inevitable that there will be a divide between those who achieve prosperity and those who do not.

Case in point: While I was in the process of connecting with others to discuss issues such as sustainability, activism, and the art of being corporately socially conscious, I met with the owner of a sixty-employee, highly profitable, privately owned company. His company's success has led to prodigious wealth for him. He was able to retire in his forties and now stays at home, taking care of his family and looking for his next project.

He decided his personal mission was to become community conscious, and he attested to believing in the principles of the Prosperity Loop: those of sharing wealth with all those who contribute to the creation of that wealth. He took pride in his having created jobs in which his employees were paid a good market wage and provided with health insurance. As a job creator, he felt he was making a significant contribution to the betterment of society.

When I asked him how his company helped support

community activism, he elaborated on how personally passionate he was about various social causes. He said that providing his employees with a paid day off each year to support volunteer work was making a real impact.

I found a lot of commonalities between this story and those of most business owners. They are amazing, talented, hardworking people who are doing the very best they can. They are extremely proud of what they have built, and they care about their employees. They have a social consciousness and usually want to contribute to the betterment of society in some manner.

But this is no longer enough. We are all aware that the world is changing—and quickly. We need to do more, be better, and surpass our previous contributions.

An increasing number of leaders are becoming aware of the choices they are being asked to accept as part of the job. They have worked long and hard in pursuing their financial success, yet they are left feeling unfulfilled and sometimes compromised. They are feeling the weight of walking among their people, and they are becoming increasingly aware that their current approach to business isn't delivering true prosperity for everyone around them—those directly contributing to the organization's success, their employees' families, and their communities.

The problem is the current economic imbalance between the "kings" and the "people." Our collective conscious is telling us that collaborative leaders and organizations need to become the new standard. Many leaders don't want to make changes unless they absolutely must because change encompasses uncertainty and potential risk and often means additional work. Change is uncomfortable for us all, and that discomfort can mean that even the best business leaders don't adapt their old business practices to the new ways of the world. When fear and discomfort creep in, it can feel easier to just keep things the way they are.

For your company to survive and thrive, your business culture needs to change. Business culture—what your company develops into both internally and within society—always *begins at the very top of an organization*. Management determines if it will be an autocracy or a collaboration of all the people who are a part of your environment. This means that how your team thinks and moves with you depends very much on how much they are respected and rewarded.

Too often, we hear statements from business leaders about how they had to "overcome challenges," "make difficult decisions," or "make choices for the betterment of the company." It's apparent to us that the actions they are taking for their businesses are of greater value to them than the people those actions impact.

Many leaders who fiercely drive to get to the top fail to notice the burdens they willingly place on others in order to reach what they consider to be the pinnacle of success. Many executives don't see that they have become a king or queen, supporting shareholder kings and queens because they were willing to "do whatever it takes" or "make significant sacrifices." This illustrates the fact that it is possible to create a cognitive dissonance that allows us to justify almost all actions we take.

Every organization's moral footprint starts with the principles and integrity of the leader and that leader's ability to dethrone him- or herself in order to walk among his or her people and come to understand them. This integrity grows through leaders' relationships with their employees, their vendors, and their customers. Morality and integrity, however, cannot be turned on and off. Every action taken and every interaction experienced has a ripple effect. If your expectations of others are different than those you have of yourself, and if what you are saying is different than what you are doing, you're off track. Realizing this requires taking an honest look at yourself. A single or small positive contribution does not outweigh a lifetime of corruption. A "king" may do something good, great, heroic, or generous in the moment, but if he is not truly the person he is portraying himself to be, the people will inevitably hope for his dethronement.

As a leader, you have most likely been put in positions that ask you to consider greater and greater levels of moral compromise, to view employees as replaceable widgets. In these positions, some will decide they will cross that line of moral compromise. Those who sacrifice their values will inevitably find a way to justify those hard choices to themselves and others. However, similar to the sense of loss associated with the death of a loved one, the sacrifice of values will always leave scars.

Conversely, imagine the impact a subtle shift in your philosophy could have on you and your employees if implemented.

This makes me think of the movie *It's a Wonderful Life,* which is so much more than a holiday tale. In Frank Capra's 1946 classic, frustrated businessman and local banker George Bailey is about to take his life when he is visited by an angel sent from heaven to help show him what the world would have been like without him and his altruism. The overarching theme of the movie is what happens when an honorable man is not around to influence a community and, instead, a greedy man is the dominant force. The message therein is one of positive influence versus negative influence. The movie serves as a great reminder about our lives and how they are so closely entwined with the lives of others. A subtler theme is the joy and happiness that is bestowed upon the good man from all of the positive relationships he has created as a result of his caring for others. It's a story many now consider antiquated or inapplicable to today's adoration of narcissism, when the opposite may, in fact, be true.

Now more than ever, we need great leaders who are willing to relate to their people, and a shift in perspective can go a long way in rebalancing our approach to valuing people. A simple adjustment to the way in which we value the people within our organizations can also change how we value ourselves and our experiences of happiness as leaders. However, this transformation, personally and organizationally, doesn't take place just by our thinking about it. It takes action to move from focusing solely on maximizing profit to accepting, valuing, rewarding, and walking among the helping hands of the organization. It takes living out the principles of the Prosperity Loop on a daily basis to build a better world.

When we choose to adopt such a model in our personal and professional lives, the blessings associated with the transition rapidly become clear. On a professional front, we build stronger, more productive companies. Within our social circles of family, friends, and community, we have the potential to create a level of collective happiness greater than what we have ever known. And within our own lives, we come to experience greater fulfillment in who we are as human beings and leaders. The Prosperity Loop presents us all with an opportunity to be at the forefront of creating a new approach to prosperity that broadens the reward system. Because if we don't see and embrace the need for us to dethrone ourselves and walk among our people, we may well end up being dethroned in a much less elegant way when the people have their say.

LEVELING THE PYRAMID

THE SOLUTION TO LEVELING THE PYRAMID must be one that is based on three fundamental moral truths:

1. All people are equal.
2. All people have value.
3. All people deserve to be respected.

These truths are the foundation of the six principles of the Prosperity Loop, which combine with the objective of a new model of business in which it is possible to increase the value of your company as you concurrently increase the value of (and for) your employees.

THE PROSPERITY LOOP

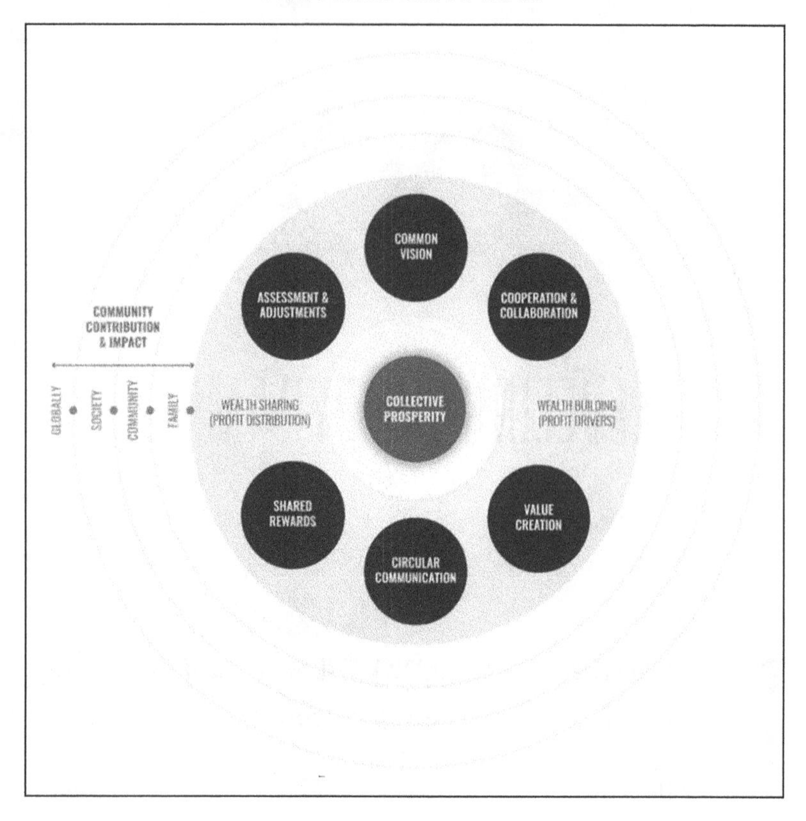

From a high-level perspective, the ultimate impact of the Prosperity Loop is a better world for you, your family, your community, society, and the whole of humanity. How we get there involves the six principles divided into two key drivers: wealth building and wealth sharing. By redefining how profit gets driven within organizations, we are positioning ourselves to more equitably distribute profits to those inside and outside our organizations in a win-win scenario.

WEALTH BUILDING AND WEALTH SHARING

What do wealth building and wealth sharing collectively entail? In a nutshell, it can be explained as "No profits means no company means no impact." Wealth needs to be created to be shared.

The interconnectedness of the six principles creates a balanced business of continual prosperity through profit building and equal (incentivized for all) profit sharing. It's important to emphasize that the processes of creating wealth and sharing wealth are not mutually exclusive; they reinforce each other. The sharing of wealth is no longer seen as a deduction from the net profit line but rather as a fuel that increases the top profit potential of the organization. Such an approach is what leads to the positive ripple effect for business owners, employees, families, communities, and society as a whole.

THE SIX PROSPERITY LOOP PRINCIPLES

Following is a high-level overview of the six principles that are going to help you achieve the distinct wealth building and wealth sharing equilibrium the Prosperity Loop is designed to achieve:

1. Common Vision

Moving a prosperous organization forward together means having a clear definition of and value in a collective corporate purpose. There are multiple approaches to achieving this, ranging from low touch to high touch. Having a common vision is ultimately about wanting to create purpose within your people by sharing in goals for the future. While such a vision often stems from the owner of the organization, it can also be built by the team as a whole. In either scenario, success comes down to created commonality by building purpose through participation. This may also involve the integration of individual visions that rally the support of a common quest.

2. Cooperation and Collaboration

You want to have valued employees at your company who have the desire to contribute to the greater whole. "Cooperation and collaboration" involves both the recognition that employees are the most important assets of any company and a dedication to creating bonds between them. It's about how you treat your most valuable assets, helping your people feel heard and respected, and having the eyes to see and ears to hear what they know about their areas of the business. As important as it is to foster cooperation and collaboration within your current employee base, it's equally important to spot the potential for cooperation and collaboration in new hires.

3. Value Creation

All those creating value for the company should be equally integrous. Value creation is about creating fundamental values within the company's culture to support collective prosperity and cohesion. This means that every employee at every level is held to the same standards because respect is a two-way street. The creation of integrity is achieved in small steps—for example, acknowledging those who dedicate themselves to delivering projects on time and conducting meetings efficiently.

4. Circular Communication

Creating a way to get honest feedback from the team is key to fostering a thriving organization where there can be prosperity for all. Circular communication is about establishing a communication model in which management and owners want to hear from all others and actively solicit feedback from their teams. Attitudes and corporate cultures are continuously evolving, and no leader should make assumptions when it comes to determining how his or her teams feel, think, or solve problems.

5. Shared Rewards

Maximization of wealth means sharing it with others, both financially and emotionally. Having shared rewards means establishing the structures through which those whose efforts made your organization what it is today are celebrated and rewarded fairly. This means creating incentives with a quantifiable financial component and some variable aspects determined by management (such as shared recognition, awards, etc.). However, the objective of any shared rewards will ultimately be the maximization of community contributions, which stems from prosperity for employees and their families.

6. Assessments and Adjustments

Traditionally, assessments are viewed as "what went wrong and how we will fix it." While any business will necessitate such action, a prosperous organization evolves assessments and adjustments to include a focus on what went right, why it did, and how things can be made even better. It involves detail-driven brainstorming to form new aspirations, with clear benchmarks with metrics to measure progress in reaching those new goals. This isn't all numbers and net gains though; the new model also involves creating heartfelt moments to celebrate people along the way—the kind of impact that cannot be measured in chart form.

There are many organizations and individuals who have successfully taken steps to create components of the Prosperity Loop. In the upcoming chapters, you will find specific stories of those who have mastered the pillars of the Prosperity Loop and detailed descriptions of what each of the six principles looks like in action. The six principles are strategically designed to provide a road map of how to build a better business, life, and community while simultaneously helping others. Each principle will help guide you and will provide relevant techniques that can be applied to the unique scope of your organization. It is my hope that by sharing these principles, gained through my decades of experience, they may serve as a guide to helping others experience a richer life in all the right ways.

THE PROSPERITY LOOP PRINCIPLES

1. COMMON VISION

DO YOU SEE WHAT I SEE? When the goals you have for your organization are not aligned with who you are as a person, there will invariably be friction. Any lacking alignment can interfere with your company's success, your happiness, your relationships, your health, and a multitude of other aspects of your life. Even greater friction can be felt when your employees have no commitment to the goals of the company or to you, as the owner. Knowing how fierce competition can be in your external market, you want to aim to create as much internal synergy and cohesion as possible in the name of strengthening your culture.

The first principle of the Prosperity Loop is the creation of a common vision, which means that, ideally, all those in the organization share a common perspective on the guiding principles and direction of where your organization is going, what it can be, and what you stand for as you work together to get there. Common vision is ultimately about creating a common purpose within your people and achieving alignment between you, your employees, and your organization's objectives. This is the source and fuel that will truly propel growth, profitability, and cultural strength.

There are several different approaches to creating a common vision, which range from low touch to high touch. A low-touch approach is based on utilizing money (donations, loans, financing) to help bond organization members via a common cause and create an impact in the community. An example is the choice to align as an organization to support community banks by making deposits designed to be used to finance projects and businesses within that local community. This approach may mean less involvement from individual employees, and one could argue that it creates less opportunity for buy-in.

Taking a high-touch approach to creating a common vision means instilling a common purpose at the individual level. The goal is to create, in all organization members, an emotional and mental stake in the company's values and direction. While shaping such a vision often stems from the owner of the organization, it can also be built by the team as a whole. In fact, there are three primary methods for shaping a common vision:

1. **Owner's Vision.** The owner leads the charge for participation around a big-picture vision.
2. **Team Vision.** The people of the company commit to a commonly formed and believed-in vision, operating as a united organization.
3. **Individualized Vision.** Small teams—regional teams, departments, or those with common charity focuses—can come together and lead with a common vision.

Let's take a deeper look at what these three models entail and the results that can be achieved by using them.

1. OWNER'S VISION

When Blake Mycoskie dropped out of Southern Methodist University in Dallas to begin a laundry business, he was labeled a "young entrepreneur." Then, on a trip to Argentina in 2006, he witnessed the hardship faced by children living without shoes. At that moment, Mycoskie evolved into a "socially conscious entrepreneur." After meeting with a group of women who talked about how they were collecting used shoes to give to children who needed them to meet the dress code in school, he knew that he wanted to be able to give shoes to those children in a sustainable way. The idea for TOMS Shoes was born, along with its unique One for One® model of donating a pair of shoes for every pair purchased. In his words, "The one-for-one model I've found is really effective in allowing a consumer to know exactly what's going to happen. There is no ambiguity; there's no crazy accounting. You buy a pair of shoes; we give a pair of new shoes to a child in need."[19]

Unsurprisingly, Mycoskie's vision led him to face great capitalistic pushback. How would he ever make money while giving away so many shoes? How would his company become sustainable? His unshakeable belief in the One for One model laid the foundation for using business to improve lives and played a key role in the development of corporate responsibility and conscious consumerism. His vision ultimately led the company to a threefold benefit:

1. **They were able to attract and retain top talent.** In its infancy, TOMS had very little money for executive salaries, yet they were able to attract top people from blue-chip companies. Many of those who joined TOMS were also extremely talented and often at the later stages of their careers. They were drawn to what TOMS stood for.

   In an Esalen Institute and Center for Theory & Research article titled "Why I started TOMS," written by Blake Mycoskie, the founder states the following:

   > *They left those corner offices and high paychecks to come join us in a warehouse office to be part of something. People want to be part of something when giving is at the core of what you're doing, especially in such a simple way as one-for-one.*[20]

   By bringing in talent whose values aligned with his company's philanthropic vision, Mycoskie and his team quickly realized another benefit to the working environment they had created. Tensions and pet peeves between employees would dissolve in the face of everyone working together toward the common vision of giving and serving a greater good, like providing shoes for children in need.

   In the above-mentioned article, Mycoskie went on to say this:

   > *When you start serving with one another, you don't worry about all the things that typically stress people out, cause lack of productivity in the company, or cause passive aggressiveness. All those things just kind of melt away when you see these*

incredible needs you're serving. So, giving is really good for attracting and retaining talented individuals, as well as for employee morale.

2. **Their customers became their marketers.** The second testament to the strength of Mycoskie's vision was the impact on its customers. "While giving feels really good, it is also an effective business strategy. . . . When you incorporate giving into your business, your customers become your marketers," he said.

   In the company's first six years, TOMS did just a small amount of online marketing and no traditional advertising. Instead of following suit with a traditional advertising strategy, the company created viral YouTube videos and let their millions of customers become their "evangelists." Hollywood stars started wearing their shoes, and TOMS gained traction, outperforming most start-ups by creatively and authentically communicating their common vision. In 2014, eight years into the business, TOMS was valued at $625 million.

3. **They attracted incredible partnerships with other organizations.** The third invaluable benefit that surfaced from TOMS operating with such strength of vision, one that Mycoskie claims was key to the company's growth and success, was the attraction of amazing partners who were drawn to the company's model of One for One giving. TOMS attracted the voluntary support of large companies, fashion designers, and individuals who stepped forth to help the company reach its next level.

> In 2009, Mycoskie got a call from AT&T. The company had heard he was a customer of theirs. They made him an offer to go on a "giving trip," for which they hired a documentary filmmaker and spent $40 million to create the largest commercial they had made in years, one that showcased how technology was helping to do good things in the world. AT&T realized more impact and results with that single commercial than they'd had with any commercial they had tested with focus groups over the previous ten years. When Mycoskie met the chairman of AT&T, he thanked him for what his company had done. The chairman then turned around and thanked Mycoskie because the joint venture and shared vision allowed AT&T to show how it was assisting a small company, such as TOMS, in helping people around the world.

Mycoskie's simple One for One vision grew into a global movement, impacting over 100 million lives. Since its launch, TOMS has partnered with countless organizations, including UNICEF, Save the Children, Partners In Health, the American Red Cross, Everytown for Gun Safety, Faith in Action, and March For Our Lives. Today, Mycoskie's original 2006 vision has evolved and continues to live on for TOMS. The company now donates both shoes and grants to children, giving away $1 for every $3 the company makes. They focus on giving to organizations that help people feel safe, well, and equal, with a vision of helping humanity to thrive. Mycoskie's clear, unshakable vision for TOMS exemplifies what can be made possible when a founder or CEO of a company has a vision around which they build their company and team.

2. TEAM VISION

Early in his career, Michael Pirron seemed like a typical consultant. For ten years, he worked as a systems consultant in the US and France with the former Andersen Consulting (now Accenture). He traveled to Israel to work as a product manager with a mobile workforce-management-solutions company and then completed his MBA from the Kellogg School of Business at Northwestern University. In his early consulting years, Pirron and his colleagues would often discuss how time and money were preventing them from doing something more fulfilling. Consulting was a lucrative profession, but it had not led Pirron and his colleagues to feel the same level of fulfillment that his friends working for nonprofits were experiencing. His vision was to form a company that would span both worlds, one that was financially lucrative and able to do good with its earnings. When Pirron founded the business and technology consulting firm Impact Makers in 2006, he did so with the mission of donating 100 percent of its lifetime value to charitable causes through its partnerships with nonprofits. The company's shared values include the following:[21]

- **Making a Difference:** Impact Makers exists for the purpose of making our local communities better.
- **Seeking Balance:** Impact Makers embraces the pursuit of balance between work, family, and personal interests.
- **Maximizing Integrity:** Impact Makers takes into account the views of all our stakeholders to ensure we are doing the right thing to maximize community impact—not just today but in the long run too.
- **Having Fun:** Impact Makers believes that work can and should be fun.

- **Honoring Commitment:** Impact Makers brings passion and enthusiasm to our work with all of our stakeholders.
- **Insisting on Quality:** Impact Makers insists that excellence and professionalism permeate the work we do for our clients and our community partners.
- **Fostering Collaboration:** Impact Makers wants our team members to feel like they work *with* Impact Makers, not *for* Impact Makers.

Pirron called the company and its vision "a sociology experiment." Together with his team, he built a consulting company with no shareholders, which was governed by a volunteer board of directors. The company's "big, hairy, audacious goal" was to be making a $1 million-a-year impact in the local communities they serve by the end of 2017.[22] By 2015, the company had reached annual revenue of $17.8 million and had donated $1 million to local charities.[23] In their first decade in business, they made over $3.7 million in direct community contributions and delivered over eleven thousand hours of pro bono services to community partners.[24]

In an interview with *Inc.* magazine, Pirron stated that the company's model (and their team vision) has helped them in three ways:

1. Their unique story has gotten them in the door for many opportunities.
2. Their vision often acted as a tiebreaker, all else being equal, in a competitive bid. In Pirron's words, "It's a group of middle-class professionals making the same impact as midsize foundations in town. That's totally disruptive."[25] Their focus on enriching the community became a competitive edge.

3. They discovered internal helpers and "voluntary salespeople" within other organizations that were prospective clients. For instance, an employee of one organization reached out to tell Impact Makers that they loved their model and wanted to help them write a proposal for that person's boss, who was the organization's CIO.

While Pirron did not list a fourth, I'd like to highlight one more way their unique model has helped them. Their clear vision helps to attract and retain talent in the highly competitive IT consulting industry. In eight years, they had just five people leave not for cause.[26]

Impact Makers has proven a new business model that tackles capitalism and benevolence at the same time. They shaped a vision for meaning and impact, and they directed that vision toward helping their community. Impact Makers co-founder Steve Wilson called their business model "a win-win opportunity for our clients, employees, nonprofit partners, and the community."[27] "We have a model that maximizes stakeholder value in the community rather than shareholder value because there are no shareholders," he said.[28]

With a team vision, a firm identifies the vision as a collective and makes a conscious commitment to unite and operate under its premise as a united organization.

3. INDIVIDUALIZED/PERSONALIZED VISION

The concept of "individualized vision" is an innovative one. It allows small teams, such as regional teams, departments, or those with common charity focuses, to come together and lead from a common vision. When it comes to identifying individualized common visions and purpose, each organization can be as creative as they want in identifying such purpose and how they are going to incite a communal commitment to it. An individualized vision can be as "micro" as a department rallying to support a colleague who has been diagnosed with cancer. It can also be more "macro," like the support of a community cause or charity that is near to the individual team's values. What's important in any case is that there is a local focus because it allows members to see the actual results of their vision and contributions. It also allows for recipients of money or pro bono work to share their stories with individual team members (e.g., during lunches or monthly celebration events). The goal of individualized vision is to have people invested in seeing how they are helping others.

When it comes to incentivization and organizational support, this model may involve empowering these individual teams to allocate their mission, time, and focus as they see best aligned with their personal visions. For some, that may mean the individual group designates a charitable contribution that is matched by the larger organization. Donations may involve minimum and maximum amounts. Typically, organizations match donations at a ratio of 1:1, though they can go higher or lower. The donations can be structured in similar fashion to a firm's matching of individual employees' IRA contributions.

Fundraising software and support company MobileCause (now part of GiveSmart) released a report titled "15 Companies with Groundbreaking Matching Gift Programs." The report highlights the top gift-matching companies, with Soros Fund Management at the top of a list that includes General Electric, Disney, Apple Inc., Boeing, and Coca-Cola, among others. Soros offers employees a 3:1 match ratio, on up to $100,000 per year. That means they are offering up to $300,000 in matching gift revenue to each of their full-time employees.[29]

In all of these vision creation and maintenance scenarios, success comes down to created commonality by building participation in forming the big-picture communication and execution of the vision. It's also important to note that none of these formation structures is mutually exclusive. For example, an owner's vision may involve the integration of individualized visions.

Whether you are starting anew or looking to make a shift from one model to another, there will inevitably be challenges to making change. If you're a CEO or manager of a small company, you are constantly being pulled into the minutiae, but your common vision must always be prioritized. We're taught to believe that if we can manage our time better, we'll get more done. The truth is that no time-management principles will help you maximize your time the way that managing your values and vision will.

This is the first and central foundation to achieving collective prosperity. Prioritizing what makes you feel happy and fulfilled, aligning vision to values, means increased opportunities to become more operationally efficient. You will be clearer on where you are going and what is required to get there. When you keep what is of value to you as a priority and communicate it with passion and clarity, your decisions will become easier (either things align with the vision or they do not), and you will attract those who are aligned with your vision (whether it is yours as the owner, your team's, or an individualized vision). When you choose to align your decisions with your values, you are sharing the decisions with other people who are aligned with those values.

You don't have to be a saint to integrate common vision into your business. Start with one small thing, such as defining a single key value, and build on that. Notice how it feels to start having a good track record. What you're focusing on is a reinforcement of the connection between happiness, values, productivity, and humanity-centric behavior. Choose to participate in allowing other people to fulfill their dreams along with your own. We need people who buy in, and the only way for them to buy in is by having them identify what is important to them. Empower purpose and vision within your workplace because, as you've seen in the stories above, where there is clear purpose and vision, attraction of talent and opportunities often becomes a natural progression.

Open your heart, mind, and eyes to being clear on your value-based direction, and do not allow yourself to get pulled in alternate directions. Taking the leap into having or creating an organization that is driven by a common vision can, in the beginning, make you feel like you are alone, a pioneer in the wild, but you are *not* alone. Remind yourself of how others, such as Blake Mycoskie and Michael Pirron, have been successful in their endeavors. Common vision doesn't need to be complex. It is simply about bringing the foundation of your business back to that which truly matters to people.

2. COOPERATION AND COLLABORATION

CAN'T WE ALL JUST GET ALONG? We each have our own unique idiosyncrasies, along with a need to have a voice and be heard. All of us want to make a difference in the world on one level or another, and we want to achieve this in ways that leave us feeling comfortable with who we are and what we are contributing to the whole.

The United States Department of Labor reported that in November 2021, workers quit their jobs in record numbers. The "quits level" surged to 4.53 million for the month, which represented an 8.9 percent increase from October and broke September's high-water mark of 4.36 million.[30] This period that saw a record number of employees quitting their jobs has been labeled the "Great Resignation." It shook many employers, further confirming the need to attract and retain talent in a more effective manner.

This is an opportunity for businesses to improve lives and build societal success. They can empower people to contribute to progress. It all comes down to how you dedicate yourself to the people who are your business. How do you identify, hire, and retain employees who buy into the common vision and whose integrity can be counted on? How do you partner with vendors and suppliers who are also aligned? For those who choose to stand clear in their vision, this is the challenge facing today's business leaders: blending the individualism of people into the collective of a team that is aligned in a common vision.

A thriving example of this philosophy is being demonstrated by Charles Koch, who founded Stand Together, a nonprofit organization based on the principles of personal empowerment. Brian Hooks is the chairman and CEO of the Stand Together Foundation, a philanthropic community that works with more than seven hundred business leaders and philanthropies to empower people to realize their unique potential and help every person rise. In their book *Believe in People,* Koch and Hooks provide real-world examples of how empowering people transforms individuals and builds teams. Based on their experience in working with thousands of organizations, they believe the following:

> At its best, business does three things. First, it empowers employees to self-actualize. Second—and as a result of the first—it develops and supplies the products and services that others use to improve their lives. Third, it helps create a culture of

> mutual benefit, in which people learn that success comes from contributing.[31]

"Cooperation and collaboration" is about how you treat your most important asset: your employees. It's about leaning in to discover what they know—and you don't—about their parts of the business. It's also about consciously bringing in new hires who align with the common vision and existing levels of cooperation and collaboration. This Prosperity Loop principle is about placing a stronger emphasis on the values and "team player mentality" of all employees, new and long-standing. This means weighing these factors with even more importance than exceptional skills alone; however, it doesn't mean hiring people who aren't fully capable. There has to be a balance between skill and alignment of values. You want to know what a team member will contribute to the collective good and the company as a whole.

Creating a Prosperity Loop involves creating an environment in which "collaboration and cooperation" becomes a more seamless, natural byproduct of daily operations rather than a series of strenuous uphill battles. It is a process that combines the mechanics of change with the values required for change. It all begins with the people who are part of your business: those you are currently working with and those you will be working with in the future.

This principle involves the recognition that employees are the most important assets of any company, as well as a dedication to creating bonds between your people. However, this isn't about kumbaya time, big, shiny financial rewards, or constantly coming together to toast marshmallows over a campfire. "Cooperation and collaboration" involves digging deeper, beyond the big picture of having a common vision as an organization in getting into the pragmatic nuts and bolts required to tie everyone together and pull that common vision into reality.

The work begins within each department, between peers and between managers and team members. From there, it can extend outward toward other departments, bringing the greater whole together in unison under the common vision. The ability of your employees to come together and participate depends on their ability to feel heard and respected. You want to work to help them feel that both of these needs are being met while making it clear that you have the eyes to see and ears to hear what they know about their areas of the business that could help fuel collective prosperity.

Of course, this presents challenges tied to individuality and individual needs. You will inevitably be working with different teams, regions, socioeconomic groups, races, and religious beliefs, and what works for one person or team may not work for others. Factored into this mix is the pandemic-induced challenge present in many businesses: creating a strong culture and drive toward a common vision in a virtual environment. It can be much harder to build bonds between people without consistent human interaction, but ultimately, the success of cooperation and collaboration begins with a common vision of having something for everyone to believe and invest in. For you in particular, as the owner, that "something" has to be your people.

PEOPLE ARE YOUR BUSINESS

For many schools, college football is a very significant business enterprise. National championship-level programs do everything in their power to identify and recruit the most talented players.

They do so for all positions, not just the quarterback or running back. To win the championship, there must also be a good coach, trainers, and practice facilities, and all parties must be able to come together to achieve the common good (the win). The bottom line is that if the players and staff aren't high quality, the ability to be a great team is significantly diminished. This reality applies not just to football teams; it also applies to every organization. Many business owners flinch at this notion since high-quality people are going to expect more in return for their talent and services. They will continue to do so, and they should, but financial compensation will be just one of the considerations among a multitude of other factors.

The America's Charities report "Snapshot Employee Research: What Employees Think about Workplace Giving, Volunteering, and CSR" states that 71 percent of employees believe it is imperative or very important to work for an employer whose missions and values align with their own.[32] The 2016 Cone Communications Employee Engagement Study found that 93 percent of people want to work for a company that cares about them as people, and 55 percent would choose to work for a socially responsible company, even if it meant a lower salary.[33] Research also supports what happens in an environment where existing employees have bought into the collective vision. PWC's report "The Keys to Corporate Responsibility Employee Engagement" finds that employees most committed to their organizations put in 57 percent more effort on the job—and are 87 percent less likely to resign—than employees who consider themselves disengaged.[34]

What is it about you, your business, your vision, your purpose, your community that will entice talent to become part of your team? Creating an environment of collective success is undeniably a big challenge. There will likely be some common hurdles, such as attachment to the way things used to be done; the protection of divisions, departments, or territories and what has historically been seen as "theirs"; cliques, communication silos, and spoken or unspoken hierarchies; along with the weight of individual personalities, idiosyncrasies, and viewpoints.

You want to be able to provide comfort and support to employees so they feel enabled to participate, to contribute, to be a part of the collective—and this is going to take some work to create. You will need to be aware of those who hide in the background and those who tend to overcontrol. Ideally, you may wish to begin with the creation of small collaborative teams that are then built and merged into the bigger picture over time once "cooperation and collaboration" has been realized at the local level. Small teams have many benefits. They can help give a platform to shy participants and, if maintained even after cooperation and collaboration efforts extend beyond the group, they can serve as a starting point. This means that small teams can hold brief meetups before larger meetings in order to be clear on their meeting objectives (and have each of their voices contribute to the desired objectives).

HIRING TEAMS BUILT FOR COOPERATION AND COLLABORATION

Who you hire, who you retain, and who you fire are some of the most important decisions your company will make. Many businesspeople have become conditioned to view employees as fixed costs rather than valuable opportunities. Especially during times of turnover, it can be easy to get caught up in the "cost of hiring."

Values and integrity can become overlooked in the process of interviewing a potential new employee.

It's not worth having a highly talented employee at any level of the organization if they are incapable of cooperation and collaboration. A person with a negative, selfish, or defeatist attitude is literally poison to your firm. Their influence can create a cascade of "can't do" problems. They may not be able to interact evenly, or they raise concerns by creating drama or exhibiting other attention-seeking behaviors. The simplest first step in making your company great is to prevent such harmful actions.

Due to the tremendous impact of each employee on the company, it is imperative that the hiring process incorporates principle hiring practices. Once hired, your employees need to experience continued engagement and the involvement of your team members and their commitment to your vision. A true common vision is one that will be mutually beneficial to the masses, not just for a select person or group of individuals. Be sure to be clear about your vision and values from the beginning, always leading from—and hiring talent from—those foundational pillars.

Personality tests and assessments can play an important part in determining whether or not people are internally aligned with your corporate vision and values. When interviewing candidates, key questions shouldn't only be about one's success in their area of skill. It's not that competency, skills, and talent are not important; they clearly are. But if you want your company to excel, character must be evaluated if your goal is an environment of cooperation and collaboration in alignment with a common vision.

It is critical to remember that character will always be more important than competencies. Competencies can be taught and enhanced, but character cannot easily be altered. Evaluating candidates based on nonquantifiable attributes can trigger some hesitation, but there are methodologies that have high success rates in quantifying personality traits such as character and integrity. You can even create your own questions to help measure character. Of course, you want to remain cautious of any unconscious bias. Every human, regardless of his or her background, race, or gender preference, has the capacity to be trusting, caring, supportive, and collaborative.

CHOOSING YOUR PARTNERS

Achieving cooperation and collaboration is not solely about the people employed within your firm. Vendors, production partners, board members, and philanthropy partners—the charities and community organizations you choose to support—all need to be aligned with your broader common vision and come together in a spirit of mutual respect, trust, integrity, cooperation, and collaboration. Some may argue that attempting to create such an environment comes with excessive costs or that it is not possible to find vendors or suppliers willing to support a common vision. That's just not true. It might just take some additional effort to identify the right partnerships, but the synergy that is created can create a ripple effect for a more powerful societal impact. Look at TOMS and AT&T!

Virginia Community Capital was founded in 2006 as a nonprofit organization dedicated to focusing on financing affordable housing, community development, and small businesses. They have supported initiatives for mental health, children's education, and office space for small businesses.

There will always be more opportunity for prosperity when "cooperation and collaboration" is expanded to create partnerships in all facets of your business. It is a second step alongside employing those who align with your organization's common vision, those who have integrity, and those with strong moral character. Follow these guidelines and you will be well on your way to fostering an environment of cooperation and collaboration. It is also very important to remember that, as a leader, your character, integrity, passion, and commitment to the corporate vision will shape and guide the behavior and dedication of your team going forward.

From today on, build your team(s) on a foundation of respect, alignment, and integrity between team members. Regardless of the problems and challenges that a business faces, one thing is certain: Having a team that aligns with the common vision and is able to collaborate and cooperate will pay dividends (both human and professional) for a long time to come. In the words of *Believe in People* authors Charles Koch and Brian Hooks, "It's recognizing our common interests and concerns, which enables us to join together to solve common problems."[35]

3. VALUE CREATION

DOING IS THE IMPORTANT PART OF BEING. When discussing business value, many people intuitively think about the valuation or worth of a company. They think of metrics that can be measured by the price of its stock, a price-to-earnings ratio, or some combination of various quantifiable data (e.g., total revenues, margin levels, EBITA). Essentially, value is often defined as the monetary or material worth of an organization. Within the Prosperity Loop model, a company's value and its values are of equal importance. The financial well-being of the organization becomes synonymous with the personal well-being of the organization's team members. In other words, having a team with high values (along with the strength of a common vision and purpose) can lead to increasing the comprehensive value of a company. And while such factors might not be as easily measured as quantifiable data, they are no less important.

When I was at Northwestern's Kellogg School of Management learning about the benefits of the free market, any discussion of creating a "managed or sufficient" level of profitability was summarily dismissed. Companies exist to maximize profits. All objections always came back to who would be the ultimate arbitrator of how much profit is "enough."

What if a company's values are to weigh into the overall value of the company? Much like we saw with Impact Makers, clear definition and articulation of corporate values (especially when they are integrous and unique) can foster increased worth with employees, clients, vendors, and partners.

Values impact profits. The source of almost all value creation within any organization begins with leadership. As the leader, you need to be an example. It's very difficult to hold others accountable for honesty, integrity, and value creation if you are not holding yourself accountable. Integrity can be further forged within the organization by showing that you honor your organization's values and live by them on a daily basis. Show that you have buy-in and that everyone's time, energy, and ideas are of equal value.

In 1978, ice cream mogul Ben & Jerry's was formed in Burlington, Vermont, by Ben Cohen and Jerry Greenfield, with the support of their allies, including legal and accounting expert Jeff Furman. The company is a great example of an organization that is purpose oriented and has integrated their values into the way they conduct business. As described in Brad Edmondson's recount of the Ben & Jerry's story in the book *Ice Cream Social: The Struggle for the Soul of Ben & Jerry's,* "Linked prosperity" is "the simple but radical idea that when the company benefits, everything it touches should also benefit, including employees, suppliers, customers, communities, and the environment."[36]

Ben & Jerry's original vision represented the epitome of value creation for all parties involved. In *Ice Cream Social,* it is made clear that any organization with a social commitment needs to have constant devotion to the social aspect of the business since there will inevitably be challenges and distractions. At the end of the day, the company understood what it meant to operate from clear values and use them to foster value for all its contributors (and give back to all of them).[37]

It can be difficult to look at a blank whiteboard and write down not only what you want to help create in the world but also what you want from life. When it comes to declaring our own values and desires, we sometimes say that we want what we think we're *supposed* to want. It's time to dig deep and ask yourself what you really want. Are where you are now and where you are going in alignment with what you truly want? Only *you* know if the life you are living and the business you are creating are right for and true to you. What you currently have might just be perfect, and if so, it's time to take steps to treasure where you are and grow what you've planted. If you're like most people, however, you will feel there is work to be done to step into full alignment with who you want to be and where you want to go.

Once the core values for a company have been established, they need to be aligned with your own values and those of your people. Having decided that you want to be a force for positive change and prosperity, you must ask yourself the questions required to move into alignment with who and where you want to be as a leader and as an organization. Here are some questions that can guide you in aligning your values as a leader with the common vision of your company:

Personal

- What's most important to me?
- What do I care most about?
- Do I want a legacy? Am I currently shaping it?
- Is who I am beginning to align with who I want to be?

Corporate

- What is my guiding vision?
- What type of team have I created? What type do I want?
- What type of culture do I want?
- Are my people on board with the bigger vision? How can I help them to be?
- How can I best lead and engage?
- How do I prioritize and maintain the objectives and vision I have defined?
- Am I taking care of others on the team?
- How can I make things fun for everyone (again)?

Societal

- What is the current ripple effect of my organization in the local and national community?
- How are my organization and vision impacting the families of my people?
- What community consciousness exists that is important to me?
- How can I integrate more of my community's needs into my corporate vision?

You can create a common vision to guide and motivate you and your team. You'll then be tasked with building character to have a high-performance team as you establish cooperation and collaboration in identifying, partnering, and maintaining high-caliber employees, vendors, and suppliers (i.e., your highly valued assets). Using the foundation of these established principles, you'll begin to foster a values-oriented culture, with the emphasis on "values." The most important of these values is integrity.

INTEGRITY IS DESTINY

When people make integrity a key component of their lifestyle (not just the word but also the intention and behavior), it transforms who they are and the relationship they have with every human being. Life is profoundly better when integrity is a consistent element of your relationships with yourself and others. Being true to yourself and your values, in both words and action, allows relationships and commitment to a common purpose to blossom.

Committing to a life of integrity can feel overwhelming if it appears to be a monumental change in behavior. Surviving in a hyper-competitive, hyper-connected, hyper-influenced world can sometimes mean cutting corners. But integrity doesn't mean heroic perfection at all times; it means accountability for alignment with core values, even in the moments when you slip up or let something slide. There will be moments and days when we do or say something that lacks integrity. We are human, and there is no such thing as "perfect."

How do we begin to meet this challenge of value creation? Here are several initial steps that may be of immediate value to you in creating greater integrity for yourself and your organization:

1. **Establish expectations for behavior.** It's important to always be clear and honest about what can be completed, what can't, what the solution is, and when it will be delivered. It's learning about fulfilling the commitments that you make to others and yourself. When a deadline can't be met, early disclosure is important and should be encouraged, but the goal is to provide realistic delivery dates and fulfill the commitments made.
2. **Make time count.** It's not hard to convince anyone in any organization that most business meetings are inefficient. A recent survey mentioned by consulting firm Better Meetings disclosed that, on average, 37 percent of meetings start late, and 67 percent of respondents say that spending too much time in meetings and on calls distracts them from making an impact at work.[38] There are significant productivity benefits to running meetings and projects on time. Meetings can be made more efficient by attendees showing up on time, coming prepared, and concluding meetings on time.
3. **Show respect for others.** There will inevitably be times when we fall back into old habits—those that may not support productivity or fully align with the values-oriented organization. There will be times when we will struggle. How we react to the times when we fall short of our aspirations will determine the long-term viability of making this life-affirming change. You can call someone out for making a mistake, but you must understand that we're all human and mistakes can happen. The points of concern will always be the conscious misdemeanors that go against the values of the organization. HR should have

ultimate responsibility for addressing those who do not align with the rules you have established for value creation within your organization.

4. **Reward success when it shows up.** Remind people why they are being asked to go above and beyond to further value creation within your organization. Show them that their efforts are acknowledged, but also remember that success doesn't always look or feel victorious. Sometimes good behavior can be disagreeable or uncomfortable when a new perspective positively changes the course (in better alignment with corporate values). You can establish a monthly meeting that allows your people to provide examples of their positive experiences, thereby acknowledging the successes of their peers.

Want to supercharge your firm's productivity and integrity? Apply the approach of "Say what you'll do and do what you say" to projects and other assigned tasks. If a sales rep says a deal will close by Friday, then that deal needs to *close* on Friday. It's time for you and everyone in your organization to start living within the commitments you have made. Take the necessary steps toward achieving alignment between commitments (what you say you will do) and results (what you do).

Learning to live with integrity takes time, but you can prepare for the process by following a few simple steps that can help one learn to do almost anything new:

- Make a commitment.
- Know you are going to stumble at times.
- Have a positive attitude and faith that you can succeed.
- Learn from your mistakes.

- Use additional resources to learn and improve.
- Practice.
- Celebrate whenever you make progress.

Companies are nothing more than the collaborative efforts and values of their employees. For this reason, it is critical to account for collective values as a major factor in overall value creation. While the level of value created from these factors may be less quantifiable, you could use the clarity and acceptability of a firm's principles and standards of behavior as a measure. When executing in alignment with the objective of value creation for the organization, team members will likely become increasingly committed to their own words and the words of their teammates. They will want to maintain the cultural integrity. Together, you will begin to collectively stand taller in your *value* and your *values* because a purpose or vision is only as strong as the integrity of those who uphold it.

When you act with integrity and have a team with integrity, collaboration and productivity are bound to rise. There is an expectation that all team members will be positive and reinforce one another's convictions. Values are like muscles: with practice, they become stronger and easier to build. Shared values give you the power to flex the muscles of your common vision within and beyond your organization. The power of your reinforced vision comes from a collective agreement of behavior that everyone exhibits and buys into in the name of continuously strengthening your truest "value proposition."

4. CIRCULAR COMMUNICATION

CAN ONE PERSON CONTROL EVERYTHING? No, nor should that be a possibility. Everyone ultimately has an imprint on everything that occurs in and influences organizational culture. The value of having circular communication is in being able to hear and learn from one another for the betterment of the whole (collective prosperity). This principle focuses on creating the mechanisms for feedback and insight in order to further reinforce buy-in in the organization's common vision, collaboration, and value creation.

Others have the power to teach us things we don't know and help us see things in a way we may never have seen them. In order to capitalize on this opportunity, companies implementing the Prosperity Loop recognize the need to shift away from the old model of business, which was often built on top-down management decision-making (where employees were directed, spoken to, or told) without the back-and-forth feedback that is so critical to effective circular communication.

In *Believe in People,* authors Charles Koch and Brian Hooks state the following:

> The "logic" behind top-down control is that the smartest people can design a program that will make everything right. Adherents to this idea truly believe they have the best knowledge, enabling them to create a one-size-fits-all formula capable of fixing anything. They may not come right out and say it, but it is clear from their actions.[39]

In relation to the old model's organizational chart, they go on to say this:

> Progress happens from the bottom up. By bottom up, I simply mean that the combined efforts of millions of people, each using their unique knowledge and abilities, are what improve the world. Every person can make a difference, and everyone has something to contribute.[40]

Over the years, companies have established processes of soliciting employee feedback, and they should be acknowledged for taking steps to provide a channel of communication with employees. Many have employed anonymous surveys or the age-old suggestion box. In more modern times, organizations have adopted 180-degree surveys and 360-degree evaluations (designed to give insightful feedback to participants from multiple sources).

While the input can be easily provided (e.g., by checking a box), it is uncommon for participants to feel engaged or as though their comments are going to have an impact. Those whose input did have an impact may never know that things changed or how their insights may have contributed to that change.

There is another side to the old checkbox input system. While this method does elicit feedback, it is unidirectional, there may be fear involved, and there may be a disconnect between the individual providing input and the input itself (due to anonymity). How different could the feedback and input process become if private chat rooms or other forums were used to hold open discussions on pressing topics requiring solutions?

Those dedicated to the Prosperity Loop know that the solving of organizational problems can only occur (and continue) when management is sensitive to the human element. Some employees will need more nurturing to willingly share their authentic opinions. In addition, conflict may occur when perspectives are openly shared. Resolving conflicting opinions about what works or does not work, or what should or should not progress, takes attentiveness and an open ear. It means finding ways to ensure that all parties feel heard while respecting the opinions of others. A collective voice can only be formed when all parties feel they have been heard and that their feedback has been accounted for. Whether ideas are contributed or discarded, there must be circular feedback to the employees as to why. Help them to grow and gain new perspective so that their future ideas become further refined.

Transparency builds loyalty and trust. That's why it is critical to integrate into a circular communication model built with the objective of fostering collective prosperity—the type of success that is only possible with input and buy-in from the members of the organization. This means having continuous circular conversations on both an employee-to-employee level and an employee-to-management level. Such a nonjudgmental communication model, whether formal or informal, is designed to be more of a loop than the top-down and bottom-up models.

If you want employees to participate in making your company better, then you have to provide the methods, incentives, and rewards for participation. The Prosperity Loop model requires not just a shared level of communication but also a shared level of opportunity and respect. What matters with the construction of any circular communication loop is that the objective will be to allow people to do the following:

- Become more involved in decision-making.
- Have the opportunity to be recognized and rewarded for their insights and contributions.
- Experience and provide greater openness and authenticity in communication.
- Offer feedback in a manner that doesn't stigmatize or blacklist participants.
- Provide insight as to why certain choices are made and directions are taken by management (particularly to those whose input was involved in the process).

Consider the impact of opening up the lines of two-way and multidirectional communication in response to the need to receive honest feedback from the entirety of your team.

CREATING A COMMUNICATION LOOP

In 2017, researchers Allan Lee, Sara Willis, and Amy Wei Tian published an article titled "Empowering Leadership: A Meta-analytic Examination of Incremental Contribution, Mediation, and Moderation," in which they examined the impact of "empowering leadership" on employee work behavior. They examined the results of 105 studies, which included data from more than thirty thousand employees from thirty countries. Their goal was to determine "whether an empowering leadership style was linked to improved job performance." They also tested whether the theory was true of different types of performance, such as routine task performance, organizational citizenship behavior, and creativity. In addition, they explored several mechanisms that could explain how empowering leadership could improve job performance and whether the impact of empowering leadership was the same across different cultures, industries, and employee experience levels.[41]

Their findings included the following insights:

1. Empowered leaders are more effective at influencing employee creativity and citizenship behavior (i.e., behavior that is not formally recognized or rewarded, like helping coworkers or attending work functions that aren't mandatory) than performing routine tasks.
2. By empowering their employees, these leaders are also more likely to be trusted by their subordinates, compared with leaders who do not empower their employees.
3. Leaders who empower their employees are more effective at influencing employee performance in Eastern (as opposed to Western) cultures, and they have a more positive

impact on employees who have less experience working within their organizations.[42]

Never assume that you know how your team feels or what the pulse of the entire company is, particularly if it is multi-cultural. Attitudes and cultures are constantly changing, and every aspect of your organization is a living, breathing evolving organism.

Here are some effective ways to build greater circular communication within your organization:

1. **Start with management.** The owners must want to hear from others and must solicit advice. Lead by example and encourage the same behavior in all team members.
2. **Take morning walks around the office.** At any time of day (though morning is usually best), senior management can walk around the office to speak with others and solicit input on a one-on-one basis. Ask questions such as "What would you do to help make our company better?"
3. **Hold "lunch mash-ups."** These free weekly lunches with employees can serve to encourage conversation and input generation. In them, employees have lunch with someone who is not in their department (and someone they don't know well). Together, the pair can share insights about current challenges their departments are facing and provide each other with ideas. There may be predetermined questions or topics to help guide the conversations. These forums should be established as places of nonjudgment and include encouragement for participants to learn about each other on a personal level as well. The teams should be encouraged to share with management the organizational ideas that are generated.

4. **Ask for employee suggestions.** Actively seek input from your employees with regard to how they want to communicate with others and provide input.
5. **Reward those who make good suggestions (such as those who help the company make money or save money).** Valuable suggestions should receive a financial reward based on how much additional net income they create for the company. There may also be an annual bonus based on contributions. Of course, there needs to be a minimum value based on the level of impact. The goal of any reward should ultimately be to get people thinking about how to make the company better and encourage them to proactively participate in doing so.
6. **Use anonymous internal polls or posting boards (so long as the anonymity does not lead to negativity).** Designate a member of your human resources team to monitor and respond to comments.

Employees want to know that their feedback is viable, valuable, and being considered or utilized. Feedback from your team is critical, and being out of touch is like an infection: It will likely continue to get worse unless addressed. You want to have a verifiable metric to determine how people within the organization are thinking and make the system transparent to build the loyalty and trust of a thriving organization.

ADDRESSING THE HUMAN ELEMENT

Nonjudgmental communication is essential when it comes to the success of circular communication. A person or group might have a perspective that is often not fully supported by all of the team members. Where differing perspectives exist, people often identify a "Position A" and an opposing "Position B." A compromise is often viewed as existing somewhere in between these two points, with both sides having to sacrifice to find the right level of agreement. The reality is that both sides have a bottom line and may not be willing to sacrifice. Ask them what that point of untouchable compromise is and why because it is often not where they think it is. They may not be as opposed to the other perspective as they'd thought. There may even be opportunities for mutual support and education.

Identifying the options that were discussed within a group and taking the time to understand how and why that perspective has been created can provide insights as to what the underlying challenge a person or group is trying to address. Understanding the core concerns of others allows for the ability to build bridges around those "cannot touch" areas. Through the building of bridges, we create a rebalancing of the scales and can begin to level the pyramid.

McKinsey & Company partners and experts Aaron De Smet, Caitlin Hewes, and Leigh Weiss say the following in their 2020 article titled "For Smarter Decisions, Empower Your Employees":

> The key to achieving better delegated decisions is to empower employees by developing their managerial capabilities to give them the authority or power to act. It's easy to tell employees what decisions they can or can't make, but our research says that this alone is not enough. Empowerment requires managers to give their employees both the tools they need to make high-quality decisions and the right level of guidance and involvement from above as they do so.[43]

You can use circular communication as a platform to foster not just collective prosperity but also the expansion of perspectives and even possibility. However, this does not take place simply as a result of one's having asked the right questions. Ultimately, successful communication is about truly hearing and understanding what is being said.

There are no strides too small when it comes to opening up the lines of honest communication. What matters is building an environment toward a company where everyone in the organization feels he or she can hear and be heard. Attitudes and company cultures are continuously evolving, and no leader wants to make assumptions when it comes to knowing how his or her team feels, thinks, or solves problems. You want to know the pulse of your employees and be sure they know the pulse of the organization as a whole. Give your people opportunities to contribute to the conversation, to provide feedback, and to be active participants in building an organization in which collective prosperity reigns.

5. SHARED REWARDS

ALL TOGETHER NOW! People need to feel both involved and appreciated to strive toward a greater, more comprehensive sense of fulfillment. Without it, employees can be left feeling as though they are in a constant state of competition, needing to be better heard and better rewarded.

Financial compensation is one of the most immediate and tangible forms of reward you can provide to your people; however, financial compensation alone is not enough, and rewards are not always financial in nature. It's what compensation represents that is so powerful. "Shared rewards" represents the desire of you, as a leader, to recognize and reward those who contribute value to your organization. It is the next step after you have established a common vision and an environment of collaboration and cooperation, created an environment in which shared values are leading to greater value, and founded a model for circular communication. The objective of sharing the profits is to create an exceptional culture formed by people who are recognized as exceptional and whose goals are to perform brilliantly. Keep in mind that recognition can go beyond just individuals and can include teams, departments, or other groupings. It all helps to collaboratively create pride and financial security for employees, friends, family, and community members.

The Prosperity Loop principle is as much about increasing the profit of your company as it is about increasing the income of every contributor who has helped to make your organization what it is today. In fact, it is the shared experience of rewarding people's contributions that will further bond your employees, fostering greater collective success.

When we look at the results of making collective prosperity the focus, we see stories such as that of PayPal president and CEO Dan Schulman, who decided in 2018 to employ a worker survey to determine whether or not his employees were able to make ends meet. Because the company paid its people above-market rates, he was expecting a positive result. To Schulman's surprise, the survey revealed that more than two-thirds of call center and entry-level employees were struggling to pay their bills each month. They weren't even able to put money aside for the future or save for emergencies. As a result, PayPal and JUST Capital instituted the Worker Financial Wellness Initiative—a program designed to make worker financial well-being a C-suite priority.[44], [45] Schulman explained, "Our mission as a company is to democratize financial access" and that while PayPal's focus had been to achieve this mission for customers, its employees were being left behind. By better understanding the financial health and security of his workers, Schulman was able to evaluate the broader implications of his mission and make critical changes to ensure that workers were not simply the purveyors of this mission but also its beneficiaries.[46]

Greater collective productivity will not occur unless rewards are shared throughout an organization. Many companies still don't comprehend this reality. In 2021, the *New York Times* reported that the Associated Press and Equilar's 2020 survey of CEO compensation identified that CEOs received 274 times the pay of the median employee at their companies. Additionally, CEO pay jumped 14.1 percent for the year, while the median workers' income increased 1.9 percent.[47]

There are too many examples of this disparity to list, but here are a few: Boeing, which had a disastrous 2020 after grounding its 737 Max aircraft following deadly crashes, announced plans to lay off thirty thousand employees after reporting a loss of $12 billion. Nevertheless, the CEO was rewarded with $21.1 million in compensation.[48] Norwegian Cruise Line barely survived the first year of the pandemic, with the cruise industry brought to a standstill. The company lost $4 billion and furloughed 20 percent of its staff, yet it more than doubled the pay of Frank Del Rio, its president and CEO, to $36.4 million.[49] At Hilton hotels, nearly a quarter of the corporate staff were laid off, and the company lost $720 million. It was reported that its president and CEO, Chris Nassetta, received $55.9 million in compensation.[50] It's hard to believe that this was the same year in which our frontline workers were pleading to be justly rewarded for their bravery.[51]

Skewed compensation levels can create negative consequences and have become a tremendous source of discontent within many organizations. However, there is even more to the picture than the monetary lack of equilibrium. In her 2020 book *Trampled by Unicorns: Big Tech's Empathy Problem and How to Fix It*, tech industry veteran Maëlle Gavet highlights the psychopathy of tech CEOs and what she believes needs to be done to change an industry and companies that have mistreated their employees.[52] In a 2020 *New York Post* article, she advocates for a more empathetic approach to rewarding employees.[53] In her words, companies "need to hire differently, promote differently, reward differently." She states, "I'm an optimist, but I'm also a capitalist. I believe there are ways to make a company more empathetic, more reasonable, a force of good in the world. And I believe in the long run, that would actually be beneficial for the businesses."

Sharing the rewards is not an insurmountable challenge. It is an opportunity for business owners and managers to create value in themselves, their companies, and their communities. Many companies are adding incentives that reward people without burdening the organization with a fixed overhead that prevents them from growing. Some include dinner with the boss or an opportunity to work from home. Remember that rewards are not just about money; they are also about shared recognition. However, in a world where many of the working class are struggling to make ends meet on a day-to-day basis, financial rewards are often necessary at the onset. Increasing compensation can have an immediate positive impact on employees' lives. Of course, you want to be strategic, as you don't want to burden your company with high fixed costs, and it is very difficult to reduce the amount of financial rewards once a policy has been established. Ideally, you can create incentives with a quantifiable financial component and some variable aspects determined by management (such as shared recognition, awards, etc.).

Here are some of the solutions that are commonly employed today:

1. **A living wage (or more).** Better salaries and benefits can create a commitment to the firm's vision. Paying a living wage is critical to creating a more just form of capitalism. JUST Capital founder and CIO Paul Tudor Jones II emphasized that "paying a living wage is the first great step to reducing the inequality gap, taking care of employees, and hopefully building a larger pie for the entire country."[54]
2. **Bonus payments.** Cash incentives, whether flexible or discretionary, can be based on preestablished objectives. They can provide an additional incentive for buy-in and collective effort. The one caveat is that any objectives need to be those that further align the team with a common goal. The goal must be achievable, and all employees need to participate in a significant manner. Bonuses can be paid out for the month, quarter, or year. They can be paid from a potential "rainy day fund" created within the organization, or flexible cash disbursements can be paid out to address the concerns associated with higher fixed costs of salary increases. It is very important to give cash payments (and a $50 gift card is never going to be a true incentive).
3. **Matched cash contributions.** Matching is one of the most powerful ways to have employees place value on being a member of the organization, particularly when the match is a multiple of the employee contribution. Cash contributions may be matched to many causes, including charitable organizations. This practice further reinforces the collective effort and helps make your people feel like you are "in it" with them.

4. **Stock grants and discounted stock purchase plans.** When structured properly, these can provide a number of positive benefits. In the February 2017 report titled "Having a Stake: Evidence and Implications for Broad-based Employee Stock Ownership and Profit Sharing," Rutgers University School of Management and Labor Relations professors Joseph R. Blasi and Douglas L. Kruse, alongside Harvard's Herbert Ascherman Chair in Economics, Richard B. Freeman, concluded there are four key reasons to have stock ownership and profit-sharing plans:
   i. Employee share ownership and profit sharing can increase worker pay and wealth and broaden the overall distribution of income and wealth. . . . To be a tool for reducing inequality, employee stock ownership and profit sharing must be spread more widely and meaningfully than it is today.
   ii. Employee share ownership and profit sharing provide incentives for more effort, cooperation, information sharing, and innovation that can improve workplace performance and company productivity.
   iii. Employee share ownership and profit sharing can save jobs by enhancing firm survival and employment stability, with wider economic benefits that come from decreasing unemployment.
   iv. Employee share ownership and profit sharing can create more harmonious workplaces with greater corporate transparency and increased worker involvement in their work lives through access to information and participation in workplace decisions.[55]

5. **Tuition allowances.** Tuition support can be extremely meaningful for employees. This direct investment in your people often provides the greatest return of all. As they grow through their education, be sure to pay them more and give them greater responsibilities.
6. **Low-interest, short-term loans.** Loans can help employees be able to address family emergencies or better navigate tough economic times.
7. **Elimination of noncompete agreements.** These are expensive to enforce, if even possible. Why not consider showing your appreciation for your employees by doing away with them? A better approach is to work to ensure your talent would prefer to stay as opposed to leaving.
8. **Incentivized community contributions.** For example, if there is a group-giving project on the table, have monthly lunches with those who benefit from the program. Recipients will be able to share how the firm and its employees have changed their lives. This will help create emotional rewards for your people.

These options for shared rewards are not just theoretical ideas. They can be seen in action at small to midsize companies such as Zevia, Verisys, and Imprivata. California-based Zevia is a leader in zero-calorie, naturally sweetened beverages. They pride themselves on offering their employees stock options and express the importance of "creating a culture like no other." They provide bonuses, 401K matching, and stock options for their people.[56] Verisys, a Virginia-based provider of data and technology platforms to health-care and workforce management organizations, offers their employees a host of additional benefits, including comprehensive medical and dental care (with an employer-funded deductible), 401K matching, a generous holiday and PTO schedule, flexible remote work plans, competitive tuition reimbursement, and even subsidized transportation passes.[57] Massachusetts-based digital identity company Imprivata has often been ranked among the "best companies to work for," which they claim is the result of their values of mutual respect and recognition for a job well done. Employees enjoy benefits such as 80 percent coverage for health care, which allowed one employee to successfully undergo IVF and bring a child into the world.[58]

The objective of any shared rewards should ultimately be the maximization of collective impact, which stems from prosperity for employees and their families. This means allowing the value created by the contributors to flow beyond the walls of the company (or the C-suite) and into the hands of your people, their families, the community, and the rest of society.

6. ASSESSMENTS AND ADJUSTMENTS

STAY FOCUSED! There will always be challenges in business. Maintaining the ability to stay in full alignment with your common vision and values, fostering cooperation and collaboration as well as circular communication, and continuously evaluating the impact of your shared rewards are not exceptions to this rule. What creating a Prosperity Loop requires will necessitate some personal application and ongoing diligence. As you work through your myriad daily detailed decisions and potential distractions, it can be very helpful to establish a series of metrics and benchmarks to keep you on point toward collective prosperity.

The question that arises is, "How do you measure prosperity?" The good news is that there are measurable financial benefits to creating a company with purpose, and those metrics can be tracked. Similar to reviewing your financial performance, "assessments and adjustments" is about creating a systematic approach to monitoring the fulfillment of goals.

You've heard mention of them already in this book, and JUST Capital is an institution living and breathing what "assessments and adjustments" for the collective good truly means. In 2013, a group of concerned people from the world of business, finance, and civil society co-founded the not-for-profit 501(c)(3) registered charity JUST Capital. These co-founders include billionaire hedge fund manager Paul Tudor Jones II, acclaimed alternative medicine and wellness leader Deepak Chopra, attorney and corporate executive Rinaldo Brutoco, media tycoon Arianna Huffington, former Goldman Sachs partner and Wall Street veteran Paul Scialla, and founder of a global strategic advisory firm Alan Fleischmann. The organization's mission is to "build an economy that works for all Americans by helping companies improve how they serve all their stakeholders—workers, customers, communities, the environment, and shareholders."[59]

JUST Capital focuses its work on "measuring what matters" by focusing on the issues that matter most to Americans. By defining what people believe is a "just business" in our modern world, they then set metrics to track and analyze these issues. The company's independent, data-driven approach brings realism to the belief that you and every leader can indeed help make the world a better place by, as the company states, "working to move the vision of stakeholder capitalism from rhetoric to reality."

As of 2022, they have polled over 160,000 Americans and established measurements for large companies that can also be utilized by smaller organizations. Every year, JUST Capital ranks among the top one hundred most "just" companies. As compared to other Russell 1000 peers, the following is true of the JUST 100 companies (as of 2021):

- They pay 18 percent more to their median workers.
- They are 4.7 times more likely to have condoned a gender or race/ethnicity pay equity analysis.
- They give six times more to charitable causes.
- They emit 86 percent fewer tons of PM2.5 emissions.
- They had a 7.2 percent higher return on equity.
- They use 123 percent more green energy.
- They had a 56 percent higher shareholder return over the past five years.[60]

I had the opportunity to sit down with JUST Capital's founding CEO and twenty-five-year veteran of the sustainable business space, Martin Whittaker. While Whittaker spends his days positively influencing some of the largest companies in the country, he is also a small-business owner who grew up in a working-class family (they lived in the North of England, near South Manchester, not far from where the Industrial Revolution started). His background and day-to-day give him a uniquely educated perspective with which to relate to the owner of any small organization seeking the blueprint to shape (or continue shaping) a just company (one with shared rewards and prosperity for all).

While JUST Capital's research and data target the companies of the Russell 1000 Index, Whittaker told us that any company can be a just company (with just behavior and a just mindset), regardless of its size or structure. He told us he believes the framework for thinking about business is universal, spanning across industries, leadership, and types and sizes of organizations. He noted that companies have common elements with a human component:

They have money (investors). They have customers (or so we hope). They use material, energy, or power (environmental impact). And the community is where the company exists in a physical sense.

When it comes to staying on track, everything circles back to the common vision and values that your stakeholders have and staying aligned with those. Whittaker says that the best way to stay in touch with this vision and values is to continuously ask your stakeholders what those things that matter *are.* At JUST Capital, the public decides their values. In an outside-in approach, they use their public polls and surveys to lead their internal direction and focus. What matters to the people is what matters to them.

According to Whittaker, in order to maintain your focus on and dedication to the Prosperity Loop, being a just company, and putting all stakeholders first, it all comes back to having a central framework. His hope is that in five to ten years, there will be a universal framework for all organizations to access. In the meantime, he stresses the importance of "doing things right." There is no quick fix. Whittaker was authentic in proclaiming that there are very few clear and obvious ways for business owners to create a path that works when it comes to honoring stakeholder capitalism and socially conscious visions. It is an evolving science and art form. He says the most important thing he has learned is to meet any business (and the people therein) where they are. You must determine what makes the most sense for you, figure out what best practice looks like, discover what other businesses are doing, and learn from them.

As the leader of a nonprofit built from scratch, Whittaker and his team of forty employees face challenges similar to those of any other small organization. He noted that any organization becoming "just" and supporting collective prosperity is about shaping a better way to do business and ensuring the continuum of that. Of course, tough choices and trade-offs will always exist. "There will be moments where you have to lay people off. There will be moments when you have to make a tough call between investing in a new product or a new business area. You don't have limitless resources," he said. This is why having a core framework and values is so important. When everything else gets stripped away, this is what is permanent.

Whittaker says that the best action you can take is to have an annual assessment process with multiple elements (surveys, focus groups, etc.) that gives you the confidence that you are focusing on the things that matter. The very point of creating a Prosperity Loop is to have a perpetual positive influence as part of your business model. While every business invariably needs assessments to fix what is not going well, this work is equally about focusing on what went right, why things went well, and how you can make them even better. How can you multiply the positive?

Assessments are an opportunity to collectively brainstorm and create even bigger and better dreams, ones in which everyone thrives together. They can provide a framework or platform for others to share their voices—whether through surveys or by providing input to the metrics or ideas for improvements. This needs to be a collective effort, not one solely controlled by management or a small group of the most vocal players.

The best questions you can ask around having an organizational framework to stay on track for meaningful success are the following:

- What is the purpose of my business?
- What will make us successful?
- What will make us sustainable?

In growing a small and/or private business that is figuring things out as it goes, you have a much greater urgency to stay on track with your vision and mission. You are also likely to have a more human feel to your environment. So much is also driven by you, as the leader. If you don't truly believe in the stakeholder-first model, no amount of external pressure or advocacy will change your mind. It will also be difficult for others in your organization to jump on board with such a mission.

When it comes to the moral imperative of being a leader with integrity, Whittaker believes that the whole area of leadership and human capital is shifting and will continue to shift further as the younger generation moves into leadership positions. He said there is a massive sea change underway, and it is difficult to measure many of these complex human and moral elements. Every CEO he's asked has had a different answer to the question of how to measure leadership integrity, purpose, and ethics. The same occurred for the question of how to tell when these elements are off course or not present at all.

Unpacking it all is a journey that begins with questions such as *What do you want to achieve? How can you do it? And how do you know if it is working (or not)?* Begin by defining the metrics that matter most to your organization, and then determine how you can measure and track them. Highlight the metrics that are moving you further into your collective potential and prosperity. Focus great effort there. See the bigger picture and try to avoid a checklist mentality. This is about more than numbers; it's about the metrics that move you further into your collective values and goals. Remember to create heartfelt moments and points of collective celebration along the way.

ACHIEVING COLLECTIVE PROSPERITY

THE PROSPERITY LOOP IS ULTIMATELY ABOUT HARNESSING THE POWER OF PURPOSE AND INTEGRITY to empower people to shift away from the harsh, everyone-for-himself, me-first perspective toward a world of enterprise fueled by equalized happiness and prosperity. This is more than adopting a pay-it-forward philosophy in which one does something nice for another person and that person goes on to do the same. The people who have helped build your organization *are* your organization. Those who have helped build your success *are* your success, and they should share in what stems from it.

The Prosperity Loop is about creating a culture of expectation for high performance, high integrity, and high reward that extends within and far beyond your organization. It is an environment where everyone who works with you and contributes to your success feels fortunate to be able to give and understand the value and impact of what they are giving. There have been significant strides made by many organizations over the years in terms of acknowledging and incorporating the contributions of all participants in a company's success. Ben & Jerry's serves as one of the first examples of a company that can succeed when profits and prosperity coexist. It is also an example of how a company's common vision and dedication to value creation will be challenged throughout its business journey.

As identified within the Prosperity Loop and the Ben & Jerry's story, the collectively determined common values and shared mission need to drive the organization forward in its pursuit of value creation and shared rewards, all the while maximizing cooperation and collaboration, along with circular communication and assessments and adjustments. There are several key practices extolled by Ben & Jerry's that beautifully summarize the primary drivers that lead to collective prosperity:

1. **Have values that are part of your culture.** Leading with values such as mutual respect, openness to others' opinions, and communal discussion is key.
2. **Clearly identify your social mission.** Specific articulation of what you stand for is required to stay focused. Once detailed, do everything possible to remain within your passion. Don't shy away from your mission because you are afraid of losing customers. The right ones will show up when you stand for being "just." There will inevitably be some tension between different missions. Recognize that as normal and embrace the differences that will arise.

You can navigate any challenges by remaining open to new ideas and encouraging input from everyone within the organization.

3. **Maintain a strong drive and commitment to the mission throughout the company.** This is particularly true if the mission is going to be a long-term commitment (which will be necessary during difficult times).
4. **Make a specific person responsible for the social mission.** It's easy to get off track with multiple hands guiding the process and the day-to-day challenges of business. Employ a lead person and be sure to have him or her gauge how likely an initiative is to succeed before moving forward with it. Always create a realistic picture of costs and benefits. Evaluate results to determine which initiatives were successful and which were not. Adjust accordingly to further the metrics that move you into collective prosperity.
5. **Extend stock sales (ownership) to all those who directly support your social mission.** While stock ownership is often reserved for employees, remember that it can also be offered to vendors and customers, similar to Ben & Jerry's offering of stock ownership to Vermont residents.
6. **Partnership with others is important.** High-value partnerships can include those with people such as the recipients of your funding and community efforts and even your suppliers. However, just like with focusing on the metrics that move you deeper into collective prosperity, everyone involved must share in the common vision. Partnerships should be made cautiously, with the understanding that this is going to be a long-term relationship.

7. **Have direct personal relationships with customers.** Much like your employees, your customers need to feel like they're a priority. Without them, there is no success. Let them stand beside you and become a part of your mission. It's great to put a face to the brand so that your company isn't an anonymous entity with unnamed customers. The closer your customer relationships, the more you can reach out to them to support your initiatives.
8. **Implement fair compensation.** Set a maximum that an executive can be paid, such as a multiple of the lowest compensation paid at the company.
9. **Make having fun part of the company culture.** Fun makes the challenges and sacrifices worth it.

May the work of the Prosperity Loop and the examples within this book lead you to redefine what true prosperity can be and understand your power to help shape it for *all* of the stakeholders within your organization.

We all talk about how we want to be "happy" or "successful," but the truth, however, is that neither of these states is an end goal. Just as obtaining wealth is not a fulfilling objective for life (despite what we may hear), happiness and true prosperity are byproducts of living and operating well—or "justly," if you will. They are a corollary spin-off derived from doing the right thing every day, in every way we can.

Business will always offer you opportunities to get caught up in the minutiae, but it also will constantly provide you with opportunities to shape a more collective, shared success. Each and every day, you can make choices that have integrity and that align with your shared values and vision. You can have a community and organizational culture that aims to make an impact on more individuals than just your executives and shareholders, and even more than just your employees. You can conduct business and live life in a manner that is based on honesty. You can choose to love and cherish your fellow human beings, bringing to light their unique contributions and impact on the collective whole. Charles Koch and Brian Hooks put it beautifully in *Believe in People:* "Success in business depends on empowering employees to succeed by contributing." That is ultimately what this book and movement are all about.

May you go forth and prosper!

ABOUT THE AUTHOR

CHRIS LAUTENSLAGER is a seasoned sales and business veteran with a master's degree in finance and economics from Northwestern University. His forty-year career spans the floors of the Chicago Mercantile Exchange, brokerages in New York City, and sales director positions in the financial, agricultural, and manufacturing industries. During his four decades in business, Chris came to witness how the very successful and extraordinary wealthy rarely gave credit to the employees who made their organizations' success a reality. On a mission to reshape the old hierarchical, shareholder-first corporate model, Chris founded

The Prosperity Loop as a proven formula for redefining the way that wealth and success are shared in American organizations and society, with the ultimate objective of increasing the collective prosperity of all Americans.

ENDNOTES

Reshaping Capitalism

1 Whipps, Heather. "How Ancient Trade Changed the World." LiveScience. Purch, February 18, 2008. https://www.livescience.com/4823-ancient-trade-changed-world.html.

2 History.com Editors. "Gilded Age." History.com. A&E Television Networks, February 13, 2018. https://www.history.com/topics/19th-century/gilded-age.

3 "Gilded Age." Wikipedia. Wikimedia Foundation, July 6, 2022. https://en.wikipedia.org/wiki/Gilded_Age#Technical_advances.

4 Friedman, Milton, Rose D. Friedman, and Binyamin Appelbaum. *Capitalism and Freedom*. Chicago: The University of Chicago Press, 2020.

5 Schumpeter, Joseph A. *Capitalism, Socialism, and Democracy*. S.l.: Aakar Books, 2021.

6 Hayes, Adam. "Adam Smith and 'The Wealth of Nations.'" Investopedia. Investopedia, July 8, 2022. https://www.investopedia.com/updates/adam-smith-wealth-of-nations/.

7 Smith, Adam. "1, Part II." Essay. In *Wealth of Nations*. New York: Classic House Books, 2009.

8 Appelbaum, Eileen, and Rosemary Batt. *Private Equity at Work: When Wall Street Manages Main Street*. New York: Russell Sage Foundation, 2014.

9 Appelbaum and Batt. *Private Equity at Work*.

10 https://americansfortaxfairness.org/tax-fairness-briefing-booklet/fact-sheet-offshore-corporate-tax-loopholes/.

11 Hamilton, Martha H. "Usury Isn't What It Used to Be." The Washington Post. WP Company, May 11, 1980. https://www.washingtonpost.com/archive/business/1980/05/11/usury-isnt-what-it-used-to-be/378a2c48-5d20-469f-aa84-b5aa67ffcafb/.

12 CreditCards.com. "How a Supreme Court Ruling Killed off Usury Laws for Credit Card Rates." Nasdaq. Accessed July 15, 2022. https://www.nasdaq.com/articles/how-supreme-court-ruling-killed-usury-laws-credit-card-rates-2010-11-12.

13 Cohen, Rob. "Why Can Credit Card Companies Charge Such High Interest Rates?" National Bankruptcy Forum, October 22, 2021. https://www.natlbankruptcy.com/why-can-credit-card-companies-charge-such-high-interest-rates/.

14 "The Lecture for The Prize Chapter 5: The Dragon Slain: The Breakup of the Standard Oil Trust." EGEE 120: Oil: International Evolution. Accessed July 15, 2022. https://www.e-education.psu.edu/egee120/node/226.

What's Essential?

15 Mirvis, Philip H. "From Inequity to Inclusive Prosperity: The Corporate Role." Organizational dynamics. Elsevier Inc., June 27, 2020. https://www.ncbi.nlm.nih.gov/pmc/articles/PMC7319911/.

16 Kinder, Molly, Laura Stateler, and Julia Du. "Windfall Profits and Deadly Risks." Brookings. Brookings, November 2, 2021. https://www.brookings.edu/essay/windfall-profits-and-deadly-risks/.

17 "About JUST Capital." JUST Capital. https://justcapital.com/about/.

18 JUST Capital. "SURVEY: What Americans Want from Corporate America During the Response, Reopening, and Reset Phases of the Coronavirus Crisis." June 2020. https://justcapital.com/reports/survey-what-americans-want-from-corporate-america-during-the-response-reopening-and-reset-phases-of-the-coronavirus-crisis/.

The Prosperity Loop Principles: Common Vision

19 Haber, Jason. "How This Company Makes Money While Making a Difference." Entrepreneur. Entrepreneur, June 9, 2016. https://www.entrepreneur.com/article/271974.
20 "Why I Started Toms: Ezine Volumes." Esalen Institute. Accessed July 15, 2022. https://www.esalen.org/ctr-journal/why-i-started-toms.
21 Brockwell, Kent Jennings. "Social Profit(Less)teers." Richmond Times-Dispatch, November 28, 2006. https://richmond.com/business/social-profit-less-teers/article_28e12376-91c7-575a-8afb-b2d8d1b89b6d.html.
22 Buchanan, Leigh. "From Corporate Consulting to Giving Away the Company Profits." Inc.com. Inc., October 13, 2014. https://www.inc.com/leigh-buchanan/inc.500-how-i-did-it-impact-makers-michael-pirron.html.
23 University of Virginia. "Impact Makers (A): The Newman's Own of Management Consulting," July 25, 2019.
24 https://www.impactmakers.com/aboutus/
25 Buchanan. "From Corporate Consulting to Giving Away the Company Profits."
26 Buchanan. "From Corporate Consulting to Giving Away the Company Profits."
27 Workmagazine Staff. "Innovators." Richmond Times-Dispatch, June 12, 2007. https://richmond.com/business/innovators/article_823a09df-a923-5cab-8a10-d80f659c28a7.html.
28 Brockwell, Kent Jennings. "A Year of Impact." Richmond Times-Dispatch, January 8, 2008. https://richmond.com/business/a-year-of-impact/article_74df3e84-5f98-5669-8e1e-f4d1247367bf.html.

29 "15 Companies with Groundbreaking Matching Gift Programs." GiveSmart, April 22, 2021. https://www.givesmart.com/blog/top-matching-gift-companies/.

The Prosperity Loop Principles: Cooperation and Collaboration

30 "Job Openings and Labor Turnover Summary," U.S. Bureau of Labor Statistics, https://www.bls.gov/news.release/jolts.nr0.htm.
31 Koch, Charles, and Brian Hooks. *Believe in People: Bottom-Up Solutions for a Top-Down World*. New York: St. Martin's Press, 2020.
32 "Snapshot Employee Research: What Employees Think about Workplace Giving, Volunteering, and CSR." America's Charities, February 25, 2022. https://www.charities.org/Snapshot-Employee-Research-What-Employees-Think-Workplace-Giving-Volunteering-CSR.
33 "2016 Cone Communications Employee Engagement Study." Cone. Accessed July 15, 2022. https://www.conecomm.com/research-blog/2016-employee-engagement-study.
34 "The Keys to Corporate Responsibility Employee Engagement." PWC, February 2014. Accessed July 15, 2022. https://www.pwc.com/us/en/about-us/corporate-responsibility/assets/pwc-employee-engagement.pdf.
35 Koch and Hooks. "Chapter Six: People Aren't Problems." In *Believe in People*, 127.

The Prosperity Loop Principles: Value Creation

36 Edmondson, Brad. "Prologue." Introduction. In *Ice Cream Social: The Struggle for the Soul of Ben & Jerry's*, xi-xiv. San Francisco, CA: Berrett-Koehler, 2014.
37 Edmondson, Brad. "Chapter One." Introduction. In *Ice Cream Social: The Struggle for the Soul of Ben & Jerry's*, xi-xiv. San Francisco, CA: Berrett-Koehler, 2014.
38 Martin, Matt. "Meeting Statistics—Stats on Costs & Time Spent in Meetings." Better Meetings, August 8, 2020. https://bettermeetings.expert/meeting-statistics/.

The Prosperity Loop Principles: Circular Communication

39 Koch and Hooks. "Chapter Six: People Aren't Problems." In *Believe in People*, 130.

40 Koch and Hooks. "Introduction: The Principles of Progress." In *Believe in People*, 3.

41 Lee, Allan, Sara Willis, and Amy Wei Tian. "Empowering Leadership: A Meta-Analytic Examination of Incremental Contribution, Mediation, and Moderation." *Journal of Organizational Behavior* Volume 39, no. Issue 3 (August 18, 2017): 306–25. https://onlinelibrary.wiley.com/doi/10.1002/job.2220.

42 Lee, Allan, Sara Willis, and Amy Wei Tian. "When Empowering Employees Works, and When It Doesn't." Harvard Business Review, August 31, 2020. https://hbr.org/2018/03/when-empowering-employees-works-and-when-it-doesnt.

43 De Smet, Aaron, Caitlin Hewes, and Leigh Weiss. "For Smarter Decisions, Empower Your Employees." McKinsey & Company. McKinsey & Company, March 1, 2021. https://www.mckinsey.com/business-functions/people-and-organizational-performance/our-insights/for-smarter-decisions-empower-your-employees.

The Prosperity Loop Principles: Shared Rewards

44 Georgescu, Peter. "Just Capital's Initiative Is Giving PayPal Workers New Hope." Forbes. Forbes Magazine, December 21, 2021. https://www.forbes.com/sites/justcapital/2021/12/17/just-capitals-initiative-is-giving-pay-pal-workers-new-hope/?sh=d0376821d4ad.

45 Clarey, Katie. "Employers Join Just Capital, PayPal in Push for Worker Financial Wellness." HR Dive, July 26, 2021. https://www.hrdive.com/news/employers-join-just-capital-paypal-in-push-for-worker-financial-wellness/603919/.

46 Tudor, Paul, and Dan Schulman. "Opinion: CEOS, Make Sure Your Employees Aren't Struggling to Get By." CNN. Cable News Network, September 22, 2020. https://www.cnn.com/2020/09/22/perspectives/employees-financially-secure-paypal/index.html.

47 Sorkin, Andrew Ross, Jason Karaian, Sarah Kessler, Michael J. de la Merced, Lauren Hirsch, and Ephrat Livni. "Behold the Highest-Paid

C.E.O.s." The New York Times. The New York Times, June 11, 2021. https://www.nytimes.com/2021/06/11/business/dealbook/ceo-highest-pay.html.

48 Gelles, David. "C.E.O. Pay Remains Stratospheric, Even at Companies Battered by Pandemic." The New York Times. The New York Times, April 24, 2021. https://www.nytimes.com/2021/04/24/business/ceos-pandemic-compensation.html.

49 Gelles. "C.E.O. Pay Remains Stratospheric."

50 Gelles. "C.E.O. Pay Remains Stratospheric."

51 Gelles. "C.E.O. Pay Remains Stratospheric."

52 Gavet Maëlle. *Trampled by Unicorns: Big Tech's Empathy Problem and How to Fix It.* Hoboken, NJ: John Wiley & Sons, Inc., 2021.

53 Spitznagel, Eric. "Why Silicon Valley CEOS Are Such Raging Psychopaths." New York Post. New York Post, September 27, 2020. https://nypost.com/2020/09/26/why-silicon-valley-ceos-are-such-raging-psychopaths/.

54 Keating, Amanda. "PayPal CEO and JUST Capital Co-Founder Discuss Worker Financial Wellness." JUST Capital. Accessed July 15, 2022. https://justcapital.com/news/paypal-ceo-and-just-capital-co-founder-discuss-why-a-healthy-economy-and-democracy-starts-with-worker-financial-wellness/.

55 Blasi, Joseph, Douglas Kruse, and Richard Freeman. "Having a Stake: Evidence and Implications for Broad-based Employee Stock Ownership and Profit Sharing." Harvard, February 1, 2017. https://www.thirdway.org/report/having-a-stake-evidence-and-implications-for-broad-based-employee-stock-ownership-and-profit-sharing.

56 "Careers with Zevia." Zevia. https://www.zevia.com/pages/careers.

57 "About Verisys." Verisys, September 23, 2021. https://verisys.com/about/.

58 Hoff, Madison. "25 Small and Midsize Companies with the Best Work Perks and Benefits." Business Insider. Business Insider, October 14, 2020. https://www.businessinsider.com/small-midsize-companies-best-perks-benefits-comparably-2020-10#6-verisys-corporation-provides-background-screening-services-and-credentialing-software-for-healthcare-providers-20.

The Prosperity Loop Principles: Assessments and Adjustments

59 "JUST Capital." Roper Center for Public Opinion Research. Accessed July 15, 2022. https://ropercenter.cornell.edu/just-capital.

60 "JUST Capital — Ranking America's Most Just Companies." JUST Capital. https://justcapital.com/.

CPSIA information can be obtained
at www.ICGtesting.com
Printed in the USA
LVHW020148211122
733505LV00019B/831/J